Sarah Bell

The British Columbia & Alberta

Adventure Travel
Guide

Guided Outdoor Trips and More

Also by Sarah Bell

The British Columbia Bed & Breakfast Guide
Also includes the Banff National Park area

The British Columbia Lodge & Resort Guide
Also includes the Banff/Jasper area and the Yukon

Gordon Soules Book Publishers Ltd.
West Vancouver, Canada
Seattle, U.S.

Canadian Cataloguing in Publication Data

Bell, Sarah.
The British Columbia and Alberta adventure travel guide

Includes index.
ISBN 1-919574-97-1

1. British Columbia—Guidebooks. 2. Alberta—Guidebooks. 3. Outdoor
recreation—British Columbia—Guidebooks. 4. Outdoor recreation—Alberta—
Guidebooks.   I. Title.
GV191.46.B75B44 1995   917.1104'4   C95-910810-6

Published in Canada by
Gordon Soules Book Publishers Ltd.
1354-B Marine Drive
West Vancouver, BC V7T 1B5
(604) 922-6588 or (604) 688-5466
Fax: (604) 688-5442

Published in the United States by
Gordon Soules Book Publishers Ltd.
620—1916 Pike Place
Seattle, WA 98101
(604) 922-6588 or (604) 688-5466
Fax: (604) 688-5442

Cover designed by Harry Bardal
Typeset by A.R. CompuType Graphics, Vancouver, BC
Printed and bound in Canada by Best Book Manufacturers

Contents at a Glance

Full contents, pages 4 to 9

Contents

Note: Italic type designates cross-reference listings

Disclaimer

Information in any guidebook is subject to change and error. It is advisable to confirm important information when making reservations.

The information contained in this book has been obtained in large part directly from the adventure travel operators listed in the book. Neither the author nor the publisher has verified the information on safety features or facilities available or any claims made by adventure travel operators in the sections titled "In the adventure travel operator's own words."

Neither the author nor the publisher accepts responsibility or liability for outdated information, omissions, errors, or unsubstantiated claims, or for any mishap, injury, or damages to person or property, or for death, involving any adventure travel operator listed in this book.

Information for Users of This Book

1. To make reservations, to confirm information, or to obtain further information, contact the individual adventure travel operators or agents. Many provide free brochures with detailed information.

2. For most of the adventure travel activities and other services, reservations are required or recommended.

3. Since many adventure travel operators offer more than one activity, it may be possible to participate in two or more activities on one trip.

4. For most of the trips, it is possible to sign up any number of people, from one person to the maximum number of people allowed on the trip.

5. Some adventure travel operators require participants to sign a waiver of liability.

6. Since different operators and agents may have different definitions of words such as "novice," "beginner," "intermediate," and "advanced," it is necessary to contact individual operators and agents for precise information on their use of these words.

7. Since different adventure travel operators may provide different items for trips described as all inclusive (or similar words), it is necessary to contact them (or their agents) for precise information on what is included.

8. For information on what to take on a specific trip, contact the individual operators (or their agents).

9. Rates are in Canadian funds and do not include applicable taxes. For information on taxes, contact the individual operators (or their agents).

10. Travel maps of British Columbia and Alberta are available from many sources, including bookstores, map stores, gas stations, other retailers, automobile associations, and government tourist information offices. (Retailers, automobile associations, and tourist information offices may obtain travel maps of British Columbia and Alberta from Gordon Soules Book Publishers Ltd. at the addresses given on the copyright page of this book.)

11. October 1997: date of change of telephone area code, in some areas of B.C., from 604 to 250.

Section 1: Guided walking, hiking, and backpacking

Purcell Lodge
ABC Wilderness Adventures Ltd.

Paul Leeson
Box 1829
Golden, BC V0A 1H0
(604) 344-2639
Fax: (604) 344-5520

Scheduled and customized guided trips and unguided trips and activities from a lodge—Purcell Lodge—accessible only by helicopter. Scheduled guided trips: walking, hiking, backpacking, heli-hiking, heli-adventures, airplane adventures, cross-country skiing, heli–cross-country skiing, ski touring, heli–ski touring, telemarking, snowshoeing, photography, and nature tours that include wildlife viewing and bird-watching. Unguided trips and activities: walking, hiking, backpacking, cross-country skiing, ski touring, telemarking, snowshoeing, photography, wildlife viewing, and birdwatching. **Location:** In the Purcell Mountains, on a remote alpine plateau with diverse terrain on the east boundary of Glacier National Park, 30 kilometres from Golden. Golden is a 75-kilometre drive west of Banff National Park. Return helicopter flight from Golden to the lodge at an additional cost. **Some highlights:** Alpine wildflower meadows, high alpine bowls, and mountain ridges with views

Section 1: Guided walking, hiking, and backpacking

of peaks and glaciers. **Level of difficulty:** All ages and levels of fitness and experience. **Time:** Summer day trips between late June and early October; winter day trips between November and April. Trips are three to seven hours. **Cost/what provided:** Guided trips, including accommodation in the lodge, $130 per person per day, based on two people per room. Group rates for accommodation only, from $55 per person per day. **Extras for additional cost:** Return helicopter flight from Golden to the lodge, cash bar, souvenirs, and sundries. **Accommodation:** Rooms in the lodge. **In the adventure travel operator's own words:** "Our spectacular and remote location is minutes by helicopter from the crowds at traditional destinations in the national parks. Come enjoy first-class hotel-calibre accommodation and experience mountain wilderness. Popular for honeymooners, clubs, groups, weddings, meetings, and corporate retreats."

Section 1: Guided walking, hiking, and backpacking

Wells Gray Park Backcountry Chalets

Box 188
Clearwater, BC V0E 1N0
(604) 587-6444
Fax: (604) 587-6446

Scheduled and customized guided hut-to-hut (two chalets and one hut) trips: walking, ski touring, and telemarking. Trips from one of the chalets: scheduled guided trips including ski touring, telemarking, randonée, and cross-country skiing; customized guided trips including walking, ski touring, telemarking, and cross-country skiing; and unguided trips including walking, ski touring, telemarking, randonée, and cross-country skiing. Scheduled and customized guided trips: wilderness canoeing. **Location:** In the Cariboo Mountains area of Wells Gray Park, near Clearwater. Clearwater is one and one-half hours' drive north of the Kamloops airport and is five and one-half hours' drive from Vancouver. The hut-to-hut system runs south to north on a 50-kilometre-long alpine plateau, in high forest and alpine areas of the park. The hut system is reached in summer by a two-hour hike and in winter either by a snowcat ride and a three-hour hike or by helicopter. Return transportation

Section 1: Guided walking, hiking, and backpacking

from Clearwater to the trailhead (a forty-five-minute drive) at no additional cost. The canoe trips are on a lake system of three lakes in the park. Return transportation from Clearwater to the first lake (a one-hour drive) at no additional cost. **Some highlights:** Alpine wildflower meadows, small peak ascents, lakes, small mammals, and the largest remaining woodland caribou herd in southern B.C. **Level of difficulty:** All levels. **Time:** Walking and canoeing trips between June and September. Skiing trips between December and April. **Cost/what provided:** All-inclusive trips, including accommodation, food, return transportation from Clearwater to the trailhead for hut/chalet trips or to the first lake for canoe trips, and guide service: $90 per person per day in summer, $110 per person per day in winter. Self-serve chalet/hut accommodation only: $30 per person per day. **Extras for additional cost:** Snowcat and helicopter transportation. **In the adventure travel operator's own words:** "Because all waste, water, and energy systems are carefully managed, our chalet system is the most environmentally sound (and comfortable) way to explore these sensitive and unique alpine regions. Experienced guides ensure that you come away with an understanding of the lakes and meadows you are exploring and the animals that live in them."

Section 1: Guided walking, hiking, and backpacking

Iskutine Lodge

Box 39
Iskut, BC V0J 1K0
(604) 234-3456

Scheduled and customized guided trips and unguided activities from a lodge with cabins—Iskutine Lodge. Guided trips: hiking; wilderness, whitewater, and flatwater canoeing and kayaking; river running; mountain biking; birdwatching; wildlife viewing; wildlife photography; airplane hiking; airplane fishing; airplane sightseeing; horseback trail riding; packhorse trips; snowshoeing; cross-country skiing; and hot springs tours. Unguided activities: wind surfing, freshwater fishing, and fly fishing. **Location:** In northwestern B.C. The lodge, surrounded by over 3.5 million acres of designated wilderness (Spatsizi and Mount Edziza parks), is 100 kilometres south of Dease Lake via the Stewart–Cassiar highway, on Lake Eddontenajon, and is reached by plane, train, car, or ferry. **Some highlights:** Volcanoes and wildlife. **Level of difficulty:** Participants should be reasonably fit and active. **Time:** The lodge is open year round. Scheduled trips between June and September. Customized trips: call for information. **Cost/what provided:** $150 to $200 per person per day, all inclusive. Includes cabin and use of lodge facilities immediately before and after each trip. **Accommodation:** In the lodge and cabins. **In the adventure travel operator's own words:** "Small group size, excellent gear for many types of activities, true wilderness setting, uncompromising conservation standards, state-of-the-art nutrition, and devoted guides mean incomparable value."

Section 1: Guided walking, hiking, and backpacking

Taste of Wilderness Tours

Terry Deamer
Box 795
Grande Cache, AB T0E 0Y0
(403) 827-4250

Scheduled and customized guided trips: hiking, backpacking, ski touring, and heli–ski touring. **Location:** In the northern Rocky Mountains, near Grande Cache. Return transportation from Grande Cache to trip's starting point at no additional cost. **Level of difficulty:** Various fitness levels, ages, and abilities. **Time:** Day trips and three-day trips. **Cost/what provided:** Hiking and backpacking day trips, $34 to $39 per person, including guide service, food, and return transportation from Grande Cache to starting point of trip. Hiking and backpacking three-day trip, $189 per person, including guide service, food, tents, sleeping mats, cooking equipment, and return transportation from Grande Cache to starting point of trip. Skiing trips: call for information. **Extras for additional cost:** Camping equipment for rent. **Accommodation:** Tent camping on three-day trips. **In the adventure travel operator's own words:** "The emphasis of our trips is on wilderness and nature interpretation and appreciation, environmental awareness, and basic outdoor skills, all in a leisurely, relaxed, no-pressure atmosphere where your safety and comfort is our number-one concern. With Willmore Wilderness Park on our doorstep, we are blessed with a wide variety of pristine mountainous terrain ideally suited to a number of outdoor pursuits."

Section 1: Guided walking, hiking, and backpacking

Island Sauvage Guiding Company Ltd.
Other trips offered by this adventure travel operator, pages 42 and 55

Lorraine Redpath
131 Beech Street
Campbell River, BC V9W 5G4
(604) 286-0205   Fax: (604) 287-8840
Toll-free: 1-800-667-4354

Scheduled and customized guided trips: hiking, hiking/sea kayaking combination, heli-hiking, nature walks, biking (including whale watching and caving excursions), heli-surfing, surfing, and whale watching/sea kayaking/caving/heli-hiking/beach walking combination. Surfing course. **Location:** Vancouver Island. Return transportation from Campbell River or other places on Vancouver Island (depending on trip) at no additional cost. **Level of difficulty:** Various levels of fitness and experience. **Time:** Between June and August. One-day and seven-day trips. **Cost/what provided:** Nootka Island/West Coast Trail hiking trip: $675 per person, including floatplane flights, meals, and guide service. Brooks Peninsula hiking trip: $775 per person, including floatplane flights, meals, and guide service. Bedwell/Clayoquot hiking and sea kayaking trip: $850 per person, including floatplane flight from trail end to Flores Island, kayak and equipment, meals, and guide service. Heli-hiking trip to various destinations: variable rates, including helicopter flights, meals, and guide service. Nature walks: $60 per person, including snacks and guide service. Biking trip: $600 per person, including equipment escort van, whale watching cruise, caving excursion, meals, camping, and guide service. Nootka Island heli-surfing trip: $850 per person, including helicopter flights, base camp, meals, and guide service. Raft Cove surfing safari trip: $350 per person, including meals, base camp, and guide service. Learn to surf weekend course: $250 per person, including equipment, camping, meals, guide service, and instruction. Combination trip with whale watching, sea kayaking, caving, heli-hiking, and beach walking: variable rates, including hotel accommodation, transportation, meals, and guide service. Return transportation from Campbell River or other places on Vancouver Island (depending on trip) at no additional cost. **In the adventure travel operator's own words:** "Vancouver Island will surprise you with wild West Coast hiking, wilderness sea kayaking, vast fields of glacial snow, and countless untouched beaches. Getting there is half the fun. Many of our trips use air access—planes or helicopters—to allow our guests to go to the most spectacular remote settings."

Section 1: Guided walking, hiking, and backpacking

Blaeberry Mountain Lodge

Rainer Grund
RR 1 S16 C–8
Golden, BC V0A 1H0
(604) 344-5296

Scheduled and customized guided and unguided trips from a lodge—Blaeberry Mountain Lodge. Guided trips: hiking; whitewater, wilderness, and flatwater canoeing and kayaking; dog sledding; heli-skiing; horseback riding; river rafting; paragliding; and gliding. Unguided trips: mountain biking, swimming, fishing, cross-country skiing, snowboarding, and downhill skiing. **Location:** In the Rocky and Purcell mountains. The lodge is 16 kilometres west of Golden. **Some highlights:** Black bears, coyotes, and elk. **Extras for additional cost:** Mountain bike and canoe rentals. **Accommodation:** Rooms in the log house lodge, from $25 per person. Bed and breakfast, from $35 per person. Half rates for children under thirteen. The whole lodge, for groups of up to ten people, $850 per week. Camping, from $10 per person. The lodge has a sundeck. **In the adventure travel operator's own words:** "Participate in spectacular adventure travel trips and activities and enjoy a stay in our spacious log house lodge, with its quiet location and wonderful views of the Rocky and Purcell mountains."

Section 1: Guided walking, hiking, and backpacking

Mount Revelstoke and Glacier National Parks

313 Third Street West
Mail: Box 350
Revelstoke, BC V0E 2S0
(604) 837-7500
Fax: (604) 837-7536

Scheduled guided trips: hiking, walking, and nature study. Customized guided trips with local private guides: river rafting, whitewater kayaking and canoeing, caving, mountaineering, and ski touring. Unguided trips and activities: hiking, mountaineering, backcountry camping, ski touring, and ski-mountaineering. Alpine huts and backcountry shelters. A full-service lodge—Glacier Park Lodge. Campgrounds. **Location:** Glacier National Park (1,350 square kilometres) and Mount Revelstoke National Park (260 square kilometres) in the Columbia Mountains between Golden and Revelstoke. **Some highlights:** Protected wilderness parks with steep mountains, glaciers, alpine wildflower meadows, alpine lakes, deep snow, grizzly bears, and caribou. **Level of difficulty:** Easy strolls; strenuous hikes; difficult climbing, skiing, and glacier crossings. **Time:** Guided trips between late June and early September. Other activities in season. **Cost/what provided:** Adult park day pass $3. Summer, winter, and annual passes available. Adult ski-touring day pass $5. Adult guided walk $2. Adult guided hike $7. Other guided trips: call for rates. Seniors' and children's rates. Visa, MasterCard. **Extras for additional cost:** Evening interpretive program, $2 per person. Seasonal and special events: call for information. **Accommodation:** The full-service lodge is at Rogers Pass in Glacier National Park. Campground, $13 per campsite per night. Backcountry camping, $2 per person per night. Backcountry huts and shelters, $10 per person per night. **More information:** Yoho, Banff, Jasper, and Kootenay national parks are within three hours' drive to the east. **In the adventure travel operator's own words:** "A visit to spectacular Mount Revelstoke and Glacier national parks will offer a memorable experience, whether you're seeking high mountain adventure, a relaxing family holiday, or an opportunity to discover and learn more about the Columbia Mountains."

Section 1: Guided walking, hiking, and backpacking

Cathedral Lakes Lodge

RR 1
Cawston, BC V0X 1C0
(604) 499-5848
Fax: (604) 226-7374

Scheduled and customized guided trips and unguided activities from a lodge with a chalet and cabins—Cathedral Lakes Lodge. Guided trips: hiking and wildlife viewing. Unguided activities: rowboating and canoeing. **Location:** In the Cascade Mountains in Cathedral Park, between Manning Park and Penticton, near Keremeos. The lodge, at 2,092 metres (6,800 feet), is on an alpine lake in the park and is reached by a 25-kilometre drive from Keremeos to a base camp and then a 15-kilometre drive in the lodge's four-wheel-drive vehicle on a private road to the lodge. Return transportation from Keremeos and from the airport at Penticton to the base camp at an additional cost. **Some highlights:** Mountain goats, mule deer, coyotes, marmots, pikas, California bighorn sheep, moose, caribou, and black bears. Marked hiking trails extend from the lodge to alpine meadows, alpine lakes, and mountains. **Time:** Between June 15 and October 15. **What provided:** Trips include guide service, return transportation from the base camp to the lodge, use of boats and canoes, and meals. **Extras for additional cost:** Watercolour and photo-graphy workshops between June and September. Return transportation from Keremeos and from the airport at Penticton to the base camp. **Accommodation:** In the lodge, the chalet, and the cabins. The lodge has a sitting area with fireplace, a dining room where meals are served buffet style, a bar, and a hot tub. No smoking in the lodge.

Section 1: Guided walking, hiking, and backpacking

Kapristo Lodge

Roswitha Ferstl
1297 Campbell Road
Mail: Box 90
Golden, BC V0A 1H0
(604) 344-6048
Fax: (604) 344-6755

Scheduled and customized guided trips and activities and unguided trips and activities from a lodge—Kapristo Lodge. Guided summer trips and activities: hiking, heli-hiking, horseback riding, golf, whitewater rafting, flatwater river cruises, mountain biking, birdwatching, and photography. Guided winter trips and activities: downhill and cross-country skiing, heli-skiing, dog sledding, and snowshoeing. Unguided trips and activities: downhill and cross-country skiing, hiking, golf, mountain biking, birdwatching, and photography. **Location:** In the Rocky Mountains, near Golden. The lodge overlooks the Columbia River. **Level of difficulty:** All levels. **Time:** The lodge is open year round. Guided trips and activities between May 2 and October 20 and between December 20 and March 20. Seven- to fourteen-day guided summer trips. One- to three-day ski packages (skiing instruction not included). Customized trips: call for information. **Cost/what provided:** Seven-day guided summer trips, $1,395 to $2,040 per person; fourteen-day guided summer trips, $2,695 to $3,805 per person; includes guide service, accommodation, meals, transportation, and activities except heli-hiking. One- to three-day unguided ski packages, $75 to $465 per person, including shared accommodation, breakfast, and downhill and cross-country skiing at Whitetooth ski area. Other trips: call for rates. Trips longer than four days include return transportation from Calgary International Airport to the lodge. Visa, MasterCard. **Extras for additional cost:** Heli-hiking. **Accommodation:** The lodge accommodates up to twelve people in rooms with twin, queen-sized, and king-sized beds. Room rates for accommodation only: one person $75, two people $90 to $120. The lodge has an outdoor Jacuzzi. The lodge is a non-smoking facility; smoking outside only. **More information:** Six national parks, including Banff and Jasper, are within a day's drive from the lodge. **In the adventure travel operator's own words:** "A retreat with professionally guided and self-guided outdoor adventure opportunities for the young and not so young. Come share the Rockies with us."

Section 1: Guided walking, hiking, and backpacking

Kermodei Wilderness Tours Ltd.

Curtis Bereza
19 Egret Street
Kitimat, BC V8C 1S8
Phone and fax: (604) 639-9453

Scheduled and customized guided trips: hiking/inflatable boat combination trips, heli-hiking, and sailing. Guided activities on some trips: wildlife viewing, whale watching, hot springs tours, and saltwater fishing. **Location:** On the north coast of B.C. and on the Inside Passage near Kitimat. Return transportation from Kitimat airport to trip's starting point at no additional cost. **Some highlights:** Orca whales, sea lions, mountain goats, bears, wolves, hot springs, and a tidal lagoon. **Level of difficulty:** All levels of fitness and experience. **Time:** Year round. Five-, six-, seven-, and ten-day trips. Customized trips: call for information. **Cost/what provided:** Six-day hiking/inflatable boat combination trip, $725 per person. Five-day heli-hiking trip, $799 per person, including helicopter flight to base camp. Hiking/inflatable boat combination trips and heli-hiking trips include guide service, meals, snacks, beverages, packs, sleeping bags, mattresses, fishing gear, rain gear, and return transportation from Kitimat airport to trip's starting point. Five-day sailing trip, $695 per person. Seven-day sailing trip, $895 per person. Ten-day sailing trip, $1,195 per person. Sailing trips include guide service, meals, snacks, beverages, accommodation on board, fishing gear, rain gear, and return transportation from Kitimat airport to trip's starting point. **Extras for additional cost:** Accommodation before and after trip and fishing licences. **In the adventure travel operator's own words:** "In the spectacular setting of B.C.'s north coast, we operate a variety of wilderness expeditions designed for people of all ages and experience levels. It is our goal to provide you with a wilderness experience of the highest calibre of service, with memories that will last a lifetime."

Section 1: Guided walking, hiking, and backpacking

Cross-references

Section 2: Guided hiking with gear carried by llamas or horses

Strider Adventures

Dan Hunter and Dorothy Reeve
RR 1 Site 24 C–7
Prince George, BC V2N 2H8
(604) 963-9542
Toll-free: 1-800-665-7752
Fax: (604) 563-8622

Llama-assisted (llamas carry gear) scheduled and customized guided trips: back-country pack trips, hikes, and nature walks. **Location:** In a number of mountain ranges in northern B.C.: North Cariboo, Dezaiko, McGregor, and the Rockies. Llamas carry gear to secluded alpine lakes and meadows. Return transportation from Prince George to trip's starting point at no additional cost. **Some highlights:** Alpine wildflower meadows, glaciers, rivers, remote lakes, waterfalls, and wildlife. **Level of difficulty:** No experience required. For people of all ages who are reasonably fit. **Time:** Between June and September. Two-, three-, four-, and seven-day pack trips. **Cost/what provided:** Pack trips, from $140 per person per day. Includes return transportation from Prince George to trailhead, guide service, meals, camping equipment, and supplies. Children under seventeen half rate. Seniors' and group rates. **Extras for additional cost:** Sleeping bags for rent. **Accommodation:** Complimentary camping immediately before and after trips. **In the adventure travel operator's own words:** "Our experienced well-trained llamas enable you to enjoy a wilderness journey without the burden of a heavy backpack. Freshly prepared meals are hearty and nutritious. Comfortable small groups will suit you and our environment."

Section 2: Guided hiking with gear carried by llamas or horses

Cross-reference

Rainbow Mountain Outfitting—Tweedsmuir Park; p. 75

Section 3: Guided ski-lift hiking

Cross-reference

The Edgewater—the Whistler area; p. 117

Section 4: Guided heli-hiking and airplane hiking

Canadian Mountain Holidays

Box 1660
Banff, AB T0L 0C0
(403) 762-7100
Toll-free: 1-800-661-0252
Fax: (403) 762-5879

Scheduled and customized guided heli-hiking/walking from five lodges—Adamant Lodge, Bobbie Burns Lodge, Bugaboo Lodge, Cariboo Lodge, and Gothics Lodge— accessible only by helicopter. Guided hiking/mountain biking/wilderness canoeing combination trips and guided hiking/mountaineering combination trips from two of the lodges. Lodge-to-lodge trips also available. **Location:** Mountains near Banff and Jasper national parks. Bobbie Burns Lodge is 170 kilometres southwest of Banff via Golden, B.C.; heliport is near Parson, B.C. Bugaboo Lodge is 170 kilometres south- west of Banff, via Radium, B.C.; heliport is near Spillimacheen, B.C. Cariboo Lodge is 125 kilometres southwest of Jasper National Park; heliport is 4 kilometres south of Valemount, B.C. Adamant Lodge and Gothics Lodge are 362 kilometres west of Banff via Golden and Revelstoke, B.C. Road access to Gothics Lodge; heliport for Adamant Lodge is at Gothics Lodge. **Level of difficulty:** All levels of fitness and experience. **Time:** One-day to six-day trips, depending on the lodge. **Cost:** $222 to $3,000 per person. Children's rates. Lodge-to-lodge trips, hiking/mountain biking/canoeing combination trips and hiking/mountaineering combination trips: call for details. **Accommodation:** The lodges have rooms with twin or double beds and private bathrooms. Each lodge has a living room with fireplace, a dining room, a bar, a sauna, an outdoor whirlpool, a fishing and swimming pond, a games room, an exercise room, and a retail shop. A massage therapist is in residence at each lodge. Adamant Lodge has a climbing wall. Bugaboo Lodge has tennis courts. **In the adventure travel operator's own words:** "Reach the lodge of your choice by heli- copter and explore unspoiled wilderness in a small group led by a knowledgeable guide."

Section 4: Guided heli-hiking and airplane hiking

Cross-references

Purcell Lodge/ABC Wilderness Adventures—the Purcell Mountains near Golden on the east boundary of Glacier National Park; p. 12

Iskutine Lodge—northwestern B.C.; p. 16

Island Sauvage Guiding Company—Vancouver Island; p. 18

Kapristo Lodge—the Rocky Mountains near Golden; p. 22

Kermodei Wilderness Tours—the northern coast of B.C.; the Inside Passage area near Kitimat; p. 23

Pemberton Helicopters—the Coast Mountains near Whistler; p. 44

Bracewell's Alpine Wilderness Adventures—the Chilcotin Plateau; p. 78

Assiniboine Heli Tours/Mount Engadine Lodge—the Rocky Mountains near Banff National Park; p. 85

Lake Louise Inn—Banff National Park and area; p. 115

The Edgewater—the Whistler area; p. 117

Section 5: Guided mountaineering, rock climbing, and ice climbing

Northern Lights Alpine Recreation

Kirk and Katie Mauthner
Box 399
Invermere, BC V0A 1K0
(604) 342-6042

Scheduled and customized guided trips: mountaineering, rock climbing, ice and snow climbing, glacier travel, alpine hiking, snowshoeing, randonée, and ski touring. Technical ropework (for rescue) seminars. **Location:** Wilderness areas of southeastern B.C., in the Rockies and the Purcell Mountains, near Invermere. **Level of difficulty:** Trips and seminars: introductory to experienced. Guides help participants improve their skills. **Cost/what provided:** Scheduled eight-day mountaineering trips and technical ropework seminars from $650 per person, excluding transportation, food, and equipment. Shorter and/or customized trips: call for rates. **In the adventure travel operator's own words:** "We offer trips to earnest participants seeking meaningful mountain experiences in the solitude of rugged, remote wilderness areas. Moving safely in the mountains is an art that must be learned, and, as with any art, we believe one learns by doing, not following. We enjoy personally arranging and guiding every trip, ensuring that each person's mountain experience is the best quality it can be."

Section 5: Guided mountaineering, rock climbing, and ice climbing

Cross-references

Mount Revelstoke and Glacier National Parks—Mount Revelstoke and Glacier national parks in the Columbia Mountains between Golden and Revelstoke; p. 20

Canadian Mountain Holidays—mountains near Banff and Jasper national parks; p. 27

Kumsheen Raft Adventures—near Lytton; p. 64

Canada West Mountain School (a division of the Federation of Mountain Clubs of B.C.)—southwestern B.C.; the Selkirk Mountains; the Coast Mountains; the Yukon; p. 113

The Edgewater—the Whistler area; p. 117

Section 6: Guided mountain biking and bicycle touring

Canusa Cycle Tours

Box 45
Okotoks, AB T0L 1T0
Toll-free in Canada and the U.S.: 1-800-938-7986

Scheduled and customized guided bicycle trips. Guided activities on some trips: hot air balloon rides, hiking, whitewater rafting, horseback trail rides, glider flights, and wildlife viewing. Bicycle rentals. **Location:** Most trips are in B.C., Alberta, and the Rocky Mountains of Montana, on diverse terrain: flats and gentle uphill and down-hill grades, with some serious climbs. One trip is across Canada. All trips begin and end in Calgary or Vancouver at a designated hotel; return transportation from des-ignated hotel or airport at no additional cost. **Level of difficulty:** Novice to advanced. **Time:** Most trips between early May and late September. Icefield highway bicycle trips December and April. Two-, four-, six-, and ten-day trips. Cross-Canada trip is seventy-six days. Customized trips: call for information. **Cost/what provided:** $250 to $1,240 per person, including camping and/or inns, meals, equipment, van sup-port, guide service, and return transportation from hotel or airport. Some trips also include hot air balloon rides, whitewater rafting, horseback trail rides, and glider flights. Cross-Canada trip: $3,800 per person, including meals, campground fees, van support, and guide service. Cash, cheques, money orders; no credit cards. **Extras for additional cost:** Bicycles, helmets, baby chariots, and sleeping bags for rent. Inn/motel accommodation on the cross-Canada trip. **Accom-modation:** Campgrounds or inns, depending on trip. **In the adventure travel operator's own words:** "We have offered quality moderately priced Rocky Mountain bicycle tours for seven years, using over twenty-five years' experience in the most scenic area in North America. We welcome participants from all over the world."

Section 6: Guided mountain biking and bicycle touring

WildWays Adventure Tours

1925 Highway 3
Christina Lake, BC V0H 1E2
Phone and fax: 1-800-663-6561

Scheduled and customized guided trips: mountain biking and hiking. Unguided trips and activities: kayaking, canoeing, windsurfing, and rock climbing. Bike rental. **Location:** The Kootenay-Boundary area of B.C. Trips start at Christina Lake. **Some highlights:** Old-growth cedar groves, hot springs, and wildlife. **Level of difficulty:** Easy to moderate biking and hiking. **Time:** Between May 15 and September 15. Half-day to seven-day trips. **Cost/what provided:** Day trips, from $59 per person. Longer trips, from $95 per person per day: includes guide service; van and boat back-up for mountain biking; meals; accommodation; and use of kayaks, canoes, and windsurfers. Group rates. Visa, MasterCard. **Extras for additional cost:** Return transportation from airport in Spokane, Washington. Bike rental, drum making, and rock climbing. **Accommodation:** Inns and/or camping. **In the adventure travel operator's own words:** "Explore pristine wilderness, quaint villages, and natural hot springs with our excellent local guides. Enjoy Christina Lake, B.C.'s warmest clean lake. Quality service and small groups are our specialty. Excellent for families with teens."

Section 6: Guided mountain biking and bicycle touring

Iskutine Lodge

Box 39
Iskut, BC V0J 1K0
(604) 234-3456

Scheduled and customized guided trips and unguided activities from a lodge with cabins—Iskutine Lodge. Guided trips: mountain biking; wilderness, whitewater, and flatwater canoeing and kayaking; river running; hiking; birdwatching; wildlife viewing; wildlife photography; airplane hiking; airplane fishing; airplane sightseeing; horseback trail riding; packhorse trips; snowshoeing; cross-country skiing; and hot springs tours. Unguided activities: wind surfing, freshwater fishing, and fly fishing. **Location:** In northwestern B.C. The lodge, surrounded by over 3.5 million acres of designated wilderness (Spatsizi and Mount Edziza parks), is 100 kilometres south of Dease Lake via the Stewart–Cassiar highway, on Lake Eddontenajon, and is reached by plane, train, car, or ferry. **Some highlights:** Volcanoes and wildlife. **Level of difficulty:** Participants should be reasonably fit and active. **Time:** The lodge is open year round. Scheduled trips between June and September. Customized trips: call for information. **Cost/what provided:** $150 to $200 per person per day, all inclusive. Includes cabin and use of lodge facilities immediately before and after each trip. **Accommodation:** In the lodge and cabins. **In the adventure travel operator's own words:** "Small group size, excellent gear for many types of activities, true wilderness setting, uncompromising conservation standards, state-of-the-art nutrition, and devoted guides mean incomparable value."

Section 6: Guided mountain biking and bicycle touring

Hammerhead Mountain Bike/Scenic Tours

4714 Fourteenth Street NW
Calgary, AB T2K 1J6
Phone and fax: (403) 547-1566

Scheduled and customized guided off-road mountain bike trips and sightseeing van tours. **Location:** Mountain bike trips in the Rocky Mountains in the Kananaskis area; return transportation from Calgary and Banff at no additional cost. Van tours in the Badlands, near Drumheller; return transportation from a number of locations in Calgary at no additional cost. **Level of difficulty:** A typical mountain bike trip is 22 kilometres on a variety of types of terrain and can be customized to most abilities and fitness levels. **Time:** Mountain bike day trips, between June and September, on Mondays, Wednesdays, and Fridays: trips from Calgary start at 8:00 a.m. and finish at 7:00 p.m.; trips from Banff start at 10:00 a.m. and finish at 5:30 p.m. Van day tours, between June and September, on Tuesdays, Thursdays, and Saturdays, start from Calgary at 9:00 a.m. and finish at 6:00 p.m. **Cost/what provided:** Mountain bike trips: $44 per person (maximum six people per trip), including guide service, twenty-one-speed mountain bikes and helmets, picnic lunch, and return van transportation from Calgary and Banff. Van tours: $45 per person (maximum twelve people per tour), including sightseeing—the Badlands, Horseshoe Canyon, and the Hoo Doos; three hours at Royal Tyrell Museum of Paleontology; guide service; and return van transportation from Calgary. **In the adventure travel operator's own words:** "A mountain bike trip on a narrow trail that winds its way through dense pine and evergreen forest, surrounded by the majestic peaks of the Rocky Mountains, could be regarded as mountain bike heaven. Our van tours explore a land that existed long ago—a warm, tropical environment where dinosaurs flourished, dominating the earth for millions of years. Now you can retrace the footsteps of the giant reptiles in a day-long tour to the Drumheller Badlands. Join us for a day you won't forget."

Section 6: Guided mountain biking and bicycle touring

Cross-references

Island Sauvage Guiding Company—Vancouver Island; p. 18

Kapristo Lodge—the Rocky Mountains near Golden; p. 22

Canadian Mountain Holidays—mountains near Banff and Jasper national parks; p. 27

Wilderness Adventures Unlimited—the southern Chilcotin area; the west Kootenays; p. 39

Kumsheen Raft Adventures—near Lytton; p. 64

Timberwolf Tours—the Rocky Mountain parks; the Kananaskis area; p. 90

Take-A-Hike Tours—the Bulkley Valley in the Coast Mountains between Prince Rupert and Prince George; p. 98

The Edgewater—the Whistler area; p. 117

Section 7: Guided ski-lift mountain biking

Cross-reference

The Edgewater—the Whistler area; p. 117

Section 8: Guided heli–mountain biking and airplane mountain biking

Cross-references

Pemberton Helicopters—the Coast Mountains near Whistler; p. 44

The Edgewater—the Whistler area; p. 117

Section 9: Guided cross-country skiing

Cross-references

Purcell Lodge/ABC Wilderness Adventures—the Purcell Mountains near Golden on the east boundary of Glacier National Park; p. 12

Wells Gray Park Backcountry Chalets—Wells Gray Park; p. 14

Iskutine Lodge—northwestern B.C.; p. 16

Kapristo Lodge—the Rocky Mountains near Golden; p. 22

Timberwolf Tours—the Rocky Mountains; northern Alberta; the Kootenays; p. 41

Take-A-Hike Tours—the Bulkley Valley in the Coast Mountains between Prince Rupert and Prince George; p. 98

Lake Louise Inn—Banff National Park and area; p. 115

Section 10: Guided heli–cross-country skiing

Cross-reference

Purcell Lodge/ABC Wilderness Adventures—the Purcell Mountains near Golden on the east boundary of Glacier National Park; p. 12

Section 11: Guided ski touring

Golden Alpine Holidays

Box 1050
Golden, BC V0A 1H0
Phone and fax: (604) 344-7273

Scheduled and customized guided trips and unguided activities from three lodges accessible only by helicopter. Guided trips: telemarking and lodge-to-lodge ski touring in winter and hiking and lodge-to-lodge hiking in summer. Unguided activities: walking, swimming, and photography. **Location:** In the Esplanade Range of the Selkirk Mountains. Helicopter pickup point is a forty-five-minute drive northwest of Golden. **Some highlights:** Alpine wildflowers, small summits, and alpine lakes. **Level of difficulty:** A variety of slopes and types of terrain. Low to intermediate backcountry or downhill experience necessary for skiing trips. No experience necessary for hiking. **Time:** Skiing between December and April. Hiking between July and September. Three-, four-, and seven-day trips. **Cost/what provided:** Based on number of nights accommodation: three nights, $580 per person; four nights, $685 per person; seven nights, $950 per person. Includes return helicopter flight, accommodation, meals, and guide service. Cash, cheques; no credit cards. **Accommodation:** Three lodges. Each lodge accommodates twelve people and has six bedrooms with double beds upstairs, a common room on the ground floor, and a sauna. Meals are served family style around a large table. **In the adventure travel operator's own words:** "Our three lodges are located in a pristine alpine environment accessed by helicopter only. Day traverses between lodges and the small group atmosphere combine to give guests a true wilderness experience. Top quality guides and excellent food allow everyone to enjoy the trip in comfort and safety."

Section 11: Guided ski touring

Interior Alpine Recreation Ltd.
Monashee Chalet

Adolf Teufele
Box 1528
Kamloops, BC V2C 6L8
Phone and fax: (604) 522-1239

Scheduled and customized guided trips and unguided trips and activities from a backcountry chalet—Monashee Chalet. Guided trips: backcountry skiing and backcountry hiking. Unguided trips and activities: backcountry skiing, backcountry hiking, and rock climbing. **Location:** In the Monashee Mountains, near Blue River, approximately two and one-half hours' drive north of Kamloops, on varied terrain at 1,846 metres (6,000 feet). In summer, the chalet is reached by hiking 3 kilometres (approximately forty-five to sixty minutes). In winter, the chalet is reached by skiing 14 kilometres along a trail (approximately five hours) or by riding the chalet's snowcat (approximately ninety minutes). Participants who wish to ski in with a lighter load have their packs and food supplies transported by the snowcat. **Level of difficulty:** All ages and skill levels. **Time:** Between December 15 and May 16 and between July 15 and October 15. **Accommodation:** The chalet accommodates up to fourteen people in seven sleeping compartments with futon mattresses and lofts for children. The chalet has wood heat, an electric generator for light, lanterns, an indoor shower, an outdoor toilet, and a kitchen with wood and propane stoves. Rates for the chalet between December 15 and May 16: $33 per person per day; groups of eight or more, $30 per person per day. January special, $20 per person per day. Rates for the chalet between July 15 and October 15: $14 per person per day. A gourmet package includes all meals. Children's rates.

Section 11: Guided ski touring

Cross-references

Purcell Lodge/ABC Wilderness Adventures—the Purcell Mountains near Golden on the east boundary of Glacier National Park; p. 12

Wells Gray Park Backcountry Chalets—Wells Gray Park; p. 14

Taste of Wilderness Tours—the northern Rocky Mountains near Grande Cache; p. 17

Mount Revelstoke and Glacier National Parks—Mount Revelstoke and Glacier national parks in the Columbia Mountains between Golden and Revelstoke; p. 20

Northern Lights Alpine Recreation—the Rocky and Purcell mountains near Invermere in southeastern B.C.; p. 29

Wilderness Adventures Unlimited—Mount Waddington; the Pantheon ranges; p. 39

Bracewell's Alpine Wilderness Adventures—the Chilcotin Plateau; p. 78

Canada West Mountain School (a division of the Federation of Mountain Clubs of B.C.)—southwestern B.C.; the Selkirk Mountains; the Coast Mountains; the Yukon; p. 113

Section 12: Guided ski-lift ski touring

Cross-reference

The Edgewater—the Whistler area; p. 117

Section 13: Guided heli–ski touring

Wilderness Adventures Unlimited

19311—116-A Avenue
Pitt Meadows, BC V3Y 1E4
(604) 465-9320
Fax: (604) 465-2123

Scheduled and customized guided trips: heli–ski touring, ski touring, sea canoeing, whitewater canoeing, mountain bike touring, and horseback trail riding. **Location:** Ski trips to Mount Waddington and the Pantheon ranges. Canoe trips throughout B.C., including Indian Arm, the west coast of Vancouver Island, Jervis Inlet, the Hotham Sound area, and the east Kootenays. Mountain bike touring trips to the southern Chilcotin area and the west Kootenays. Horseback trail riding trips to the east Kootenays and the Chilcotin area. Trips start in Vancouver. **Time:** Nine-day ski trips between February and May. One- to seven-day sea canoeing trips between May and September. Seven-day whitewater canoeing trips in July and August. Five- to seven-day mountain bike touring trips in July and August. Five- to seven-day horseback trail riding trips between July and September. **Cost/what provided:** Nine-day ski trips, $1,500 to $2,000 per person. One- to seven-day sea canoeing trips, $59 to $850 per person. Seven-day whitewater canoeing trips, $850 per person. Five- to seven-day mountain bike touring trips, from $650 per person. Five- to seven-day horseback trail riding trips, from $850 per person. Includes return transportation from Vancouver to trip's starting point, guide service, food, accomodation, and equipment. **In the adventure travel operator's own words:** "We specialize in expeditions from the Arctic to Antarctica, with professionally certified guides; in B.C., we arrange scheduled and customized tours to some of the finest destinations one could imagine."

Section 13: Guided heli–ski touring

Cross-references

Purcell Lodge/ABC Wilderness Adventures—the Purcell Mountains near Golden on the east boundary of Glacier National Park; p. 12

Taste of Wilderness Tours—the northern Rocky Mountains near Grande Cache; p. 17

The Edgewater—the Whistler area; p. 117

Section 14: Guided telemarking

Cross-references

Purcell Lodge/ABC Wilderness Adventures—the Purcell Mountains near Golden on the east boundary of Glacier National Park; p. 12

Wells Gray Park Backcountry Chalets—Wells Gray Park; p. 14

Golden Alpine Holidays—the Esplanade Range of the Selkirk Mountains; p. 36

Canada West Mountain School (a division of the Federation of Mountain Clubs of B.C.)—southwestern B.C.; the Selkirk Mountains; the Coast Mountains; the Yukon; p. 113

Section 15: Guided downhill skiing and snowboarding

Timberwolf Tours Ltd.
***Other trips offered by this adventure
travel operator, page 90.***

**13 Menlo Crescent
Sherwood Park, AB T8A 0R8
(403) 467-9697
Fax: (403) 467-7686**

Scheduled and customized minibus trips for the following guided activities: downhill skiing and various combinations of downhill skiing, snowcat skiing, dogsledding, and snowmobiling. Minibus sightseeing trips with the following guided activities: dogsledding, snowmobiling, horse-drawn sleigh riding, cross-country skiing, and wildlife viewing. **Location:** Trips begin in Calgary and go to the Rocky Mountains, the mountains near Revelstoke, northern Alberta, and the Kootenays. Examples of possible trips: a snowcat skiing trip to Banff National Park and the mountains near Revelstoke; a downhill skiing trip to Banff and Lake Louise; a minibus sightseeing trip to northern Alberta, the Rocky Mountains, and the Kootenays. **Time:** Between December and April. Seven- to fifteen-day trips. **Cost/what provided:** Sample rates: Ten-day snowcat/downhill skiing combination trip, from $2,925 per person. Eight-day skiing/dogsledding/snowmobiling combination trip, from $1,795 per person. Eight-day downhill skiing trip, from $1,385 per person. Trips include return transportation from Calgary, guide service, accommodation, and ski passes. **Accommodation:** Hotels and cabins. **In the adventure travel operator's own words:** "The choice of ski terrain is unlimited; there are long meadows, open bowls, steep slopes, and peak ascents. Your holiday can be an opportunity to enjoy a quiet lodge in remote wilderness and the ambience of local towns, with restaurants, clubs, and visitors from around the world."

Section 15: Guided downhill skiing and snowboarding

Cross-references

Kapristo Lodge—the Rocky Mountains near Golden; p. 22

Island Sauvage Guiding Company—Vancouver Island near Campbell River; the Coast Mountains; p. 42

Take-A-Hike Tours—the Bulkley Valley in the Coast Mountains between Prince Rupert and Prince George; p. 98

Lake Louise Inn—Banff National Park and area; p. 115

Far Side of the Mountain—various locations in B.C. and Alberta; p. 116

The Edgewater—the Whistler area; p. 117

Section 16: Guided heli-skiing and heli-snowboarding

Island Sauvage Guiding Company Ltd.
Other trips offered by this adventure travel operator, pages 18 and 55.

Lorraine Redpath
131 Beech Street
Campbell River, BC V9W 5G4
(604) 286-0205   Fax: (604) 287-8840
Toll-free: 1-800-667-4354

Scheduled and customized guided trips: heli-skiing, heli-snowboarding, downhill skiing, and snowboarding. Snowboard guide instruction courses. Avalanche awareness courses. **Location:** On Mount Cain (near Campbell River, on Vancouver Island) and on Mount Waddington (in the Coast Mountain Range). Return transportation from Campbell River to trip site at no additional cost. **Level of difficulty:** Various levels of fitness and experience. **Time:** Between December and July. **Cost/what provided:** Heli-skiing and heli-snowboarding day trip: $450 per person, including guide service, transportation, and lunch. Mount Cain seven-day downhill skiing and snowboarding trip: $1,100 per person, including transportation, hotels, heated yurt (tent) camp at Mount Cain, breakfasts, dinners, lift tickets, guide service, and instruction. Two-day powder downhill skiing camp trip: $225 per person, including transportation, Mount Cain lift tickets, guide service, powder downhill skiing instruction, meals, and heated yurt (tent) camp. Six-day Coast Range downhill skiing and snowboarding hut trip: $450 per person, including transportation from Campbell River, helicopter flight to hut, meals, guide service, and instruction. Seven-day mountain glacier base camp downhill skiing and snowboarding trip: $850 per person, including transportation from Campbell River, helicopter flight to base camp, meals, guide service, and instruction. Fifteen-day Mount Waddington downhill skiing and snowboarding trip: $1,850 per person, including transportation, flights to Upper Franklin glacier, meals, guide service, and instruction. Summer snowboard glacier camp trip: $750 per person, including transportation from Campbell River, helicopter flights to and from base camp, meals, guide service, and instruction. Apprentice snowboard guide course (January 1 to May 15, 1996): $7,500 per person, including one hundred days of instruction, participation and certification as assistant avalanche technician, snowboard instructor certificate, and advanced first aid training. Two-day avalanche awareness course: $125 per person, including lift tickets, manual, certificate, specialized equipment, and instruction. Two-day advanced avalanche awareness course with helicopter: $400 per person, including instruction, equipment, and helicopter flight. **In the adventure travel operator's own words:** "Many of our trips use air access—planes or helicopters—to allow our guests to go to the most spectacular remote settings."

Section 16: Guided heli-skiing and heli-snowboarding

Tyax Lodge Heliskiing

Box 1118
Vernon, BC V1T 6N4
(604) 558-5379
Tyax Lodge (in winter): (604) 238-2446
Toll-free: 1-800-667-4854
Fax: (604) 558-5389

Scheduled and customized guided heli-skiing and heli-snowboarding trips from a lodge—Tyax Lodge. Guided and unguided activities include snowmobiling, cross-country skiing, snowshoeing, ice skating, ice hockey, and ice fishing. Retail, repair, and rental shops. **Location:** In the southern Chilcotin mountains, north of Whistler, approximately 200 kilometres north of Vancouver. The lodge is on a lake, Tyaughton Lake, and is reached by helicopter, plane, car, or bus. Bus transportation from Vancouver or Whistler at no additional cost. **Level of difficulty:** Heli-skiing and heli-snowboarding for intermediate to expert skiers and snowboarders. Previous powder skiing experience not necessary. Powder ski instruction available at no additional cost. **Cost:** Variable rates, depending on duration and season of trip. **Group size:** Maximum of four or eleven skiers and/or snowboarders per guide, depending on trip. **Extras for additional cost:** Powder skis for rent. **Accommodation:** The lodge has single and double rooms with private bathrooms, a dining room, a lounge, a stone fireplace, a games room, a balcony, a sauna, and an outdoor Jacuzzi. **In the adventure travel operator's own words:** "Heli-skiers and snowboarders have been coming to us since 1986 to enjoy the magnificent southern Chilcotin mountains of B.C. Our operation has the perfect combination of spectacular powder skiing and luxurious Western-style lodging at a remote mountain lodge. We offer skiing through old-growth forests, glacier skiing on open slopes that run for eternity, and great powder. If these are your dreams, then this is the right place for you."

Section 16: Guided heli-skiing and heli-snowboarding

Pemberton Helicopters Inc.

Pemberton Meadows Road
Mail: Box 579
Pemberton, BC V0N 2L0
(604) 894-6919
Toll-free: 1-800-894-3919
Fax: (604) 894-6987

Scheduled and customized guided trips: heli-skiing, heli-snowmobiling, heli-fishing, heli-hiking, and heli–mountain biking. Some trips include a visit to a wilderness hot springs. **Location:** In the Coast Mountain Range, near Pemberton and Whistler. Trips start at Pemberton, 150 kilometres north of Vancouver, 35 kilometres north of Whistler. Return transportation from Vancouver and Whistler to Pemberton at an additional cost. **Time:** Heli-skiing in winter; heli-fishing, heli-hiking, and heli–mountain biking in summer. Heli-snowmobiling year round. **In the adventure travel operator's own words:** "Nestled in the magnificent setting of the Coast Mountain Range, we specialize in spectacular heli-adventures that can be combined with a secluded hot springs soak for an unforgettable experience."

Section 16: Guided heli-skiing and heli-snowboarding

Cross-references

Blaeberry Mountain Lodge—the Rocky and Purcell mountains; p. 19

Kapristo Lodge—the Rocky Mountains near Golden; p. 22

Assiniboine Heli Tours—the Rocky Mountains near Banff National Park; p. 85

Lake Louise Inn—Banff National Park and area; p. 115

Far Side of the Mountain—various locations in B.C. and Alberta; p. 116

The Edgewater—the Whistler area; p. 117

Section 17: Guided snowcat skiing and snowcat snowboarding

Selkirk Wilderness Skiing Ltd.

Brenda M. Drury
1 Meadow Creek Road
Meadow Creek, BC V0G 1N0
(604) 366-4424
Fax: (604) 366-4419

Scheduled guided downhill snowcat deep snow skiing from a lodge. Retail and rental shop. **Location:** Meadow Mountain in the Selkirk Mountain Range, 97 kilometres north of Nelson, on a variety of slopes covering 5 hectares (30 square miles) of terrain. Top elevation 2,430 metres (7,900 feet); base elevation 1,200 metres (3,900 feet). Return transportation from Nelson to the lodge at no additional cost. Transportation on a twelve-passenger snowcat to top of ski runs. **Some highlights:** Untouched snow and runs from 300 metres (975 feet) to 1,200 metres (3,900 feet). **Level of difficulty:** First-time snowcat skiers should be at least strong intermediate downhill skiers, able to ski (in control) the black diamond runs at major lift-serviced areas. Experience in deep snow conditions not necessary; guides teach novice powder skiers. Guides also help experienced skiers improve their technique. **Time:** Between mid-December and mid-April. Trip packages include five days' skiing and six nights' accommodation. Three- to five-day skiing packages available on standby basis. **Cost/what provided:** Between December 24 and January 13 and between March 17 and March 30, $2,120 per person; between January 14 and March 16, $2,440 per person; between December 17 and December 23 and between March 31 and April 13, $1,850 per person. Includes five days' skiing, six nights' accommodation; heated, enclosed snowcats; two or three guides per group of twelve skiers; deep snow instruction; all meals; and return transportation from Nelson. **Extras for additional cost:** Powder ski rentals. **Accommodation:** The ten-thousand-square-foot lodge accommodates up to twenty-four guests. The lodge has living rooms, recreation rooms, fireplaces, a sauna, an open air Jacuzzi, table tennis, pool tables, a retail shop, a ski workshop, and a rental shop. **In the adventure travel operator's own words:** "We invite you to ride in comfort to ski endless miles of untouched deep powder snow. The massive peaks and glaciers of the Purcell and Selkirk mountains provide a breathtaking backdrop for this unique wilderness experience."

Section 17: Guided snowcat skiing and snowcat snowboarding

Cross-references

Timberwolf Tours—Banff National Park; the mountains near Revelstoke; p. 41

Far Side of the Mountain—various locations in B.C. and Alberta; p. 116

Section 18: Guided snowshoeing

Cross-references

Purcell Lodge/ABC Wilderness Adventures—the Purcell Mountains near Golden on the east boundary of Glacier National Park; p. 12

Iskutine Lodge—northwestern B.C.; p. 16

Kapristo Lodge—the Rocky Mountains near Golden; p. 22

Northern Lights Alpine Recreation—the Rocky and Purcell mountains near Invermere in southeastern B.C.; p. 29

Lake Louise Inn—Banff National Park and area; p. 115

Section 19: Guided dog sledding

Cross-references

Blaeberry Mountain Lodge—the Rocky and Purcell mountains; p. 19

Kapristo Lodge—the Rocky Mountains near Golden; p. 22

Timberwolf Tours—the Rocky Mountains; the mountains near Revelstoke; northern Alberta; the Kananaskis area; p. 41

Lake Louise Inn—Banff National Park and area; p. 115

Section 20: Guided snowmobiling

Cross-references

Timberwolf Tours—the Rocky Mountains; the mountains near Revelstoke; northern Alberta; the Kootenays; p. 41

Bearhead Creek Wilderness Tours—the Peace River area; p. 80

Section 21: Guided heli-snowmobiling

Cross-reference

Pemberton Helicopters—the Coast Mountains near Whistler; p. 44

Section 22: Guided horse-drawn sleigh riding

Cross-references

Timberwolf Tours—the Rocky Mountains; the mountains near Revelstoke; northern Alberta; the Kootenays; p. 41

Big Bar Guest Ranch—the Cariboo area near Clinton; p. 74

Section 23: Guided gliding

Pemberton Soaring Centre Ltd.

Rudolf Royzsypalek and Peter Timm
Pemberton Airport
Mail: Box 725
Pemberton, BC V0N 2L0
(604) 894-5727

Scheduled and customized guided sailplane gliding flights in two-seater sailplanes. Glider pilot training available. **Location:** The Pemberton/Whistler area. Pemberton is 35 kilometres north of Whistler. Trips start at Pemberton Airport. **Time:** Between early April and mid-October. **Cost/what provided**: $70 per person for fifteen- to twenty-minute valley flight to $155 per person for one-hour glacier flight. Visa. **In the adventure travel operator's own words:** "Our aircraft and pilots are licensed by the Department of Transport. Experience the exhilaration of silent flight over some of the most breathtaking scenery in the province."

Section 23: Guided gliding

Cross-references

Blaeberry Mountain Lodge—the Rocky and Purcell mountains; p. 19

Canusa Cycle Tours—B.C.; Alberta; Montana; p. 31

Section 24: Guided paragliding

Cross-references

Blaeberry Mountain Lodge—the Rocky and Purcell mountains; p. 19

The Edgewater—the Whistler area; p. 117

Section 25: Guided sea canoeing and sea kayaking

Geoff Evans Kayak Centre

Geoff and Barbara Evans
Box 3097
Cultus Lake, BC V2R 5H6
Phone and fax: (604) 858-6775

Scheduled and customized guided sea kayaking trips. On some of the trips: guided whale watching; guided wildlife viewing; guided saltwater fishing; oyster picking; and visiting ancient Native villages, petroglyphs, and totem carvings. Instructional kayaking trips. **Location:** A number of locations in B.C., including Johnstone Strait, the Broken Islands, the Gulf Islands, and Clayoquot Sound. **Some highlights:** Minks, otters, sea lions, dolphins, seals, eagles, and deer. **Time:** Between May and August. Scheduled trips: multi-day. Customized trips: call for information. **Cost/what provided:** Approximately $100 per person per day, all inclusive. Visa. **In the adventure travel operator's own words:** "Our guides, operating since 1976, have over fifty years of combined wilderness and paddling experience in countries as far afield as England, Norway, the United States, and Mexico. Enjoy unspoiled wilderness, confident that your tour will be safe, secure, exciting, and designed to match the challenge you set for yourself amid nature's best."

Section 25: Guided sea canoeing and sea kayaking

Wild Heart Adventures

RR 4 Site P C–5
Nanaimo, BC V9R 5X9
(604) 722-3683
Fax: (604) 722-2175

Scheduled and customized guided sea kayaking trips and sea kayaking/hiking combination trips. **Location:** The waterways, islands, and inlets of Vancouver Island and surrounding area: Johnstone Strait/Robson Bight, Nootka Sound, Clayoquot Sound, the Broken Islands, the Deer Group Islands, and the Gulf Islands. Trips start from various locations on Vancouver Island. **Some highlights:** Orca whales, sea life, wildlife, and tranquil waters. **Level of difficulty:** No previous kayaking experience necessary. **Cost/what provided:** Johnstone Strait/Robson Bight trip: three days, $369 per person; six days, $649 per person. Nootka Sound trip: six days, $649 per person. Clayoquot Sound trip: five days, $499 per person. Broken Islands trip: four days, $395 per person. Deer Group Islands trip: four days, $375 per person. Gulf Islands trip: one to three days, $60 to $229 per person. West Coast sea kayaking/hiking combination trip: six days, $699 per person. Includes guide service, food, kayaks, and equipment. **In the adventure travel operator's own words:** "Our expeditions, in top-of-the-line kayaks, are aimed at anyone wild at heart and free of spirit. In addition to majestic scenery, tranquil waters, and spectacular sea life and wildlife, great food is an integral part of our expeditions. Our guides are experienced sea kayakers with wilderness first aid certification and are selected for their skill, good humour, and love of adventure. If you want to get away from it all, try something you've dreamed of doing, meet new friends, and learn something new about yourself, all amidst the splendour of British Columbia's magnificent west coast, then we invite you to treat yourself and join us on one of our expeditions."

Section 25: Guided sea canoeing and sea kayaking

Tofino Sea Kayaking Company

Dorothy Baert
320 Main Street
Mail: Box 620
Tofino, BC V0R 2Z0
(604) 725-4222
Toll-free phone and fax: 1-800-TOFINO-4

Scheduled and customized guided sea kayaking trips. Sea kayaking courses. Sea kayak rentals. **Location:** Clayoquot Sound, on the west coast of Vancouver Island. Trips begin at Tofino, three hours' drive from Nanaimo, five hours' drive from Victoria. **Time:** Between April and September. One- to six-day trips. Two- to eight-day courses. **Cost/what provided:** Day trip, $38 to $75 per person. Two-day trip, $260 per person. Three-day trip on holiday weekends, $400 per person. Four-day trip, $500 per person. Five-day trip, $620 per person. Six-day trip, $725 per person. Customized trip, $135 to $155 per person per day. Family and group rates. Trips include guide service, kayaks and equipment, meals, and camping equipment. Two-day course, from $250 per person. Three-day course, from $275 per person. Five-day course, from $500 per person. Eight-day course, from $760 per person. Courses include guide service, instruction, meals, and camping equipment. **Extras for additional cost:** Kayaks and equipment on kayaking courses. **Accommodation:** The Paddler's Inn Bed and Breakfast, in Tofino: rooms with shared bath, from $55, based on double occupancy; self-contained suite with deck, from $75 (no breakfast), based on double occupancy. **More information:** Some trips for women only. **In the adventure travel operator's own words:** "Our company was founded in 1987 and since then has been providing small groups with the joyful experience of connecting with wilderness from the unique perspective of the seaworthy kayak. We operate in Clayoquot Sound, home to the Nuu-Chah-Nulth for thousands of years and still the largest remaining intact coastal temperate rainforest in southern B.C. The waterways, inaccessible by vehicle, are an ideal paddling environment, offering miles of shoreline, inlets, islands, sand beaches, and hot springs."

Section 25: Guided sea canoeing and sea kayaking

Northern Lights Expeditions

101—6141 NE Bothell Way
Seattle, WA 98155
(206) 483-6396
Fax: (206) 483-1554

Scheduled guided sea kayaking trips for viewing marine mammals. **Location:** Northern Vancouver Island. **Some highlights:** Orcas (killer whales) and bald eagles. **Level of difficulty:** No previous kayaking experience necessary. **Time:** Six-day trips between June and September. **Cost/what provided:** $1,100 to $1,700 per person, including guide service, kayaks, equipment, and food. **Accommodation:** Tents or a lodge. **In the adventure travel operator's own words:** "Since 1983, we have organized sea kayaking adventures in the world-famous Inside Passage, noted for its beautiful landscape and abundance of wildlife including orcas and bald eagles. The guides' knowledge of wildlife, natural surroundings, and Native culture highlights the trips."

Section 25: Guided sea canoeing and sea kayaking

Ecomarine Ocean Kayak Centre

1668 Duranleau Street
Vancouver, BC V6H 3S4
(604) 689-7575
Fax: (604) 689-5926
Coastal Kayaking School: (604) 689-7520

Scheduled and customized guided sea kayaking trips. Sea kayaking lessons and sea kayaking guide instruction. Retail shop and rental shops for kayaks and outdoor equipment. **Location:** Trips take place on the west coast of B.C., including the Gulf Islands, Clayoquot Sound, Nootka Sound, and the Broughton Archipelago. Trips start at Nanaimo, Tofino, and Port McNeill. Guide courses take place in Clayoquot Sound and Nootka Sound. Retail and rental shop in Vancouver at Granville Island and rental shop in Vancouver at Jericho Beach. Retail and rental shop at Granville Island is near protected waters suitable for first-time kayakers. **Level of difficulty:** No experience required. Minimum age fifteen. **Time:** Three- to eight-day trips. Nine-day and twenty-eight-day guide instruction courses. Granville Island retail and rental shop open year round. Jericho Beach rental shop open between May 15 and September 15. **Cost/what provided:** Three-day Gulf Islands trip, $395 per person. Five-day Clayoquot Sound trip, $840 per person. Seven-day Nootka Sound trip, $1,025 per person. Eight-day Broughton Archipelago trip, $1,195 per person, including float plane flight. Nine-day guide instruction course, $955 per person. Twenty-eight-day guide instruction course, $2,995 per person. Trips and courses include guide service, instruction, meals, camping equipment, kayak, paddle and spare, sprayskirt, pump, and whistle. **Extras for additional cost:** Wetsuits, additional paddles, roofracks, and midwheels. **In the adventure travel operator's own words:** "Our wilderness programs are educational; the natural environment is our classroom. We strive to share with participants the tools they need to competently undertake their own independent sea kayaking trips. We offer participants a relaxing, fulfilling, and memorable experience."

Section 25: Guided sea canoeing and sea kayaking

Island Sauvage Guiding Company Ltd.

Other trips offered by this adventure travel operator, pages 18 and 42.

Lorraine Redpath
131 Beech Street
Campbell River, BC V9W 5G4
(604) 286-0205   Fax: (604) 287-8840
Toll-free: 1-800-667-4354

Scheduled and customized guided sea kayaking trips and sea kayaking/whale watching combination trips. Sea kayaking courses. **Location:** Vancouver Island. Return transportation from Campbell River or Tofino to trip site at no additional cost. **Level of difficulty:** Various levels of fitness and experience. **Time:** Between April and September. Half-day, four-day, eight-day, and nine-day trips. **Cost/what provided:** Half-day introductory kayaking trip, $75 per person. Four-day surf landing kayaking course, $350 per person. Eight-day Bunsby Islands base camp trip, $950 per person, including float plane flights. Eight-day Nootka Sound trip, $625 per person. Eight-day Nuchatlitz Inlet trip, $750 per person. Eight-day Robson Bight orca whale watching trip, $750 per person. Nine-day Quatsino Sound trip, $750 per person. Eight-day Brooks Peninsula trip: variable rates, including float plane flights. Trips include return transportation from Campbell River or Tofino, kayaks and equipment, meals (snacks on half-day trip), guide service, and instruction. **In the adventure travel operator's own words:** "Our guides are friendly local people with the highest professional standards. They willingly share their knowledge of this region and work hard to make your trip the best ever."

Section 25: Guided sea canoeing and sea kayaking

Cross-references

Wilderness Adventures Unlimited—the B.C. coast; p. 39

Nature Connection—the Queen Charlotte Islands; the Inside Passage of B.C.; Johnstone Strait; Robson Bight; p. 83

Nimmo Bay Heli-Ventures—northern Vancouver Island and nearby coastal mainland areas; p. 86

Hollyhock—Cortes Island in the northern Gulf Islands; p. 107

Section 26: Guided whitewater canoeing and whitewater kayaking

Cross-references

Iskutine Lodge—northwestern B.C.; p. 16

Blaeberry Mountain Lodge—the Rocky and Purcell mountains; p. 19

Mount Revelstoke and Glacier National Parks—Mount Revelstoke and Glacier national parks in the Columbia Mountains between Golden and Revelstoke; p. 20

Wilderness Adventures Unlimited—various locations in B.C.; p. 39

Nimmo Bay Heli-Ventures—northern Vancouver Island and nearby mainland areas; p. 86

Jasper Adventure Centre—Jasper National Park; p. 93

The Edgewater—the Whistler area; p. 117

Section 27: Guided wilderness canoeing and wilderness kayaking

Pathways Canada Tours

Chris Harris
Box 333
108 Mile Ranch, BC V0K 2Z0
(604) 791-6631
Fax: (604) 791-6671

Scheduled and customized guided wilderness canoeing trips. **Location:** In the Cariboo Mountains, on a 116-kilometre canoe circuit in Bowron Lake Park. Trips begin at a lodge on Bowron Lake. **Some highlights:** Glacier lakes, mountain and glacier views, and wildlife. **Level of difficulty:** For adults of all ages in good health and reasonable fitness. Guides provide canoeing instruction when necessary. **Time:** Eight-day canoe trips, between June and September. **Cost/what provided:** Eight-day trip, $1,245 per person. Includes guide service, canoes, canoe carriers, paddles, tents, cooking equipment, meals from lunch on the first day to brunch at the lodge on the last day, park fees, and reserved campsites. **Extras for additional cost:** Accommodation and meals at the lodge. **In the adventure travel operator's own words:** "Enjoy a spectacular wilderness canoe trip with friendly, knowledgeable certified guides who have led over two hundred expeditions on the Bowron Lakes. Our trips have catered to individual interests and skill levels for over twenty years."

Section 27: Guided wilderness canoeing and wilderness kayaking

Iskutine Lodge

Box 39
Iskut, BC V0J 1K0
(604) 234-3456

Scheduled and customized guided trips and unguided activities from a lodge with cabins—Iskutine Lodge. Guided trips: wilderness, whitewater, and flatwater canoeing and kayaking; river running; hiking; mountain biking; birdwatching; wildlife viewing; wildlife photography; airplane hiking; airplane fishing; airplane sightseeing; horseback trail riding; packhorse trips; snowshoeing; cross-country skiing; and hot springs tours. Unguided activities: wind surfing, freshwater fishing, and fly fishing. **Location:** In northwestern B.C. The lodge, surrounded by over 3.5 million acres of designated wilderness (Spatsizi and Mount Edziza parks), is 100 kilometres south of Dease Lake via the Stewart–Cassiar highway, on Lake Eddontenajon, and is reached by plane, train, car, or ferry. **Some highlights:** Volcanoes and wildlife. **Level of difficulty:** Participants should be reasonably fit and active. **Time:** The lodge is open year round. Scheduled trips between June and September. Customized trips: call for information. **Cost/what provided:** $150 to $200 per person per day, all inclusive. Includes cabin and use of lodge facilities immediately before and after each trip. **Accommodation:** In the lodge and cabins. **In the adventure travel operator's own words:** "Small group size, excellent gear for many types of activities, true wilderness setting, uncompromising conservation standards, state-of-the-art nutrition, and devoted guides mean incomparable value."

Section 27: Guided wilderness canoeing and wilderness kayaking

Cross-references

Wells Gray Park Backcountry Chalets—Wells Gray Park; p. 14

Blaeberry Mountain Lodge—the Rocky and Purcell mountains; p. 19

Canadian Mountain Holidays—mountains near Banff and Jasper national parks; p. 27

Timberwolf Tours—the Athabasca River system; p. 90

Jasper Adventure Centre—Jasper National Park; p. 93

Lake Louise Inn—Banff National Park and area; p. 115

Section 28: Guided flatwater canoeing and flatwater kayaking

Cross-references

Iskutine Lodge—northwestern B.C.; p. 16

Blaeberry Mountain Lodge—the Rocky and Purcell mountains; p. 19

Jasper Adventure Centre—Jasper National Park; p. 93

Lake Louise Inn—Banff National Park and area; p. 115

The Edgewater—the Whistler area; p. 117

Section 29: Guided river rafting and river running

Whitewater Rafting (Jasper) Ltd.

Mark Howe
Box 362
Jasper, AB T0E 1E0
(403) 852-RAFT(7238) or 1-800-557-RAFT(7238)
Fax: (403) 852-3623

Scheduled and customized guided river rafting trips. **Location:** In Jasper National Park, on the Athabasca, Maligne, and Sunwapta rivers. **Level of difficulty:** On the international scale for grading rivers (which ranges from an easy Class I to a very difficult Class VI), the Athabasca River is rated Class II, an introductory level with a minimum age requirement of six years. The Maligne and Sunwapta rivers provide Class III white water; there is no minimum age requirement, but participants must be physically fit and have a chest or waist size larger than 70 centimetres (27 inches). **Time:** Between May 1 and early October. One-and-one-half-hour to four-hour trips. **Cost/what provided:** From $36 per person. Children under eleven half rate on some trips. Includes guide service, wet suits, all necessary equipment, and transportation. There is a guide on each eight-person raft. Visa, MasterCard. **In the adventure travel operator's own words:** "Our river experiences range from introductory white water to some of the best commercial whitewater rafting in Canada's western national parks. The two runs on the Athabasca River provide an excellent introduction to whitewater rafting and spectacular views of the Rocky Mountains. The Maligne and Sunwapta rivers offer more thrills with superb white water and breathtaking scenery."

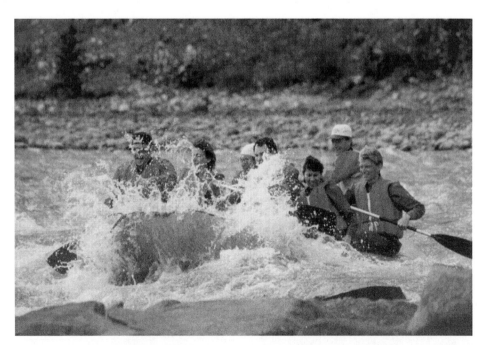

Section 29: Guided river rafting and river running

Whitewater Voyageurs Ltd.

Box 1983
Golden, BC V0A 1H0
(604) 344-7335
Toll-free: 1-800-667-RAFT (7238)
Fax: (604) 344-6688

Scheduled and customized guided whitewater rafting trips. Scheduled and customized guided river float trips. Other activities on some of the trips: guided hiking,
guided horseback riding, firewalking workshops, golf, and barbecues. **Location:** On
the Kicking Horse River in the Rocky Mountains, near Golden. **Level of difficulty:**
Beginner to experienced. **Time:** Between May and September. Half-day, one-day,
and two-day trips. **Cost/what provided:** From $44 per person, including guide ser-
vice, self-bailing boats, wetsuits, wetsuit socks and gloves, and dry bags to keep
belongings dry. Group rates. **Extras for additional cost:** Riverside campsite and
teepee rentals. **Accommodation:** Riverside campsite with teepees, hot tub, sauna,
and sweat lodge. **In the adventure travel operator's own words:** "Our government-
certified guides are trained in river rescue, first aid, and wilderness survival and specialize in river games and humour. We emphasize the harmony between humans and
nature. The river flows past the untouched wilderness of the Rockies. Time spent
observing, shooting rapids, and hiking leads to an appreciation of nature's bounty
and its fragile ecology. Go with the flow."

Section 29: Guided river rafting and river running

Wild Water Adventures

Box 25
Lake Louise, AB T0L 1E0
(403) 522-2211
Fax: (403) 522-2211

Scheduled and customized guided whitewater rafting trips. **Location:** On the Kicking Horse River in the Rocky Mountains, starting 50 kilometres west of Lake Louise. Return transportation from Lake Louise village and hotels to river at no additional cost. **Time:** Between mid-May and mid-September, starting at 8:30 a.m. and finishing at 1:00 p.m. or starting at 1:30 p.m. and finishing at 6:00 p.m. **Level of difficulty:** For first-time to experienced rafters. Good health recommended. Minimum weight 90 pounds. **Cost/what provided:** $59 per person, including guide service, wetsuits, wool/fleece sweaters, rain jackets, river shoes, helmets, gloves, return transportation from Lake Louise village and hotels to river, and pastries and beverages at end of trip. **In the adventure travel operator's own words:** "Discover one of the most exciting half-day excursions in the Banff/Lake Louise area. Enjoy frequent splashes and exhilarating rapids as you raft through the splendour of the Rocky Mountains. The qualifications and experience of our guides, together with carefully selected equipment, demonstrate that your safety is of utmost importance to us."

Section 29: Guided river rafting and river running

Canadian River Expeditions

22—1212 Alpha Lake Road
Mail: Box 1023
Whistler, BC V0N 1B0
Toll-free: 1-800-898-7238
Fax: (604) 938-6621

Scheduled and customized guided river rafting trips. Guided activities on some trips: airplane sightseeing; wildlife viewing; walking; hiking; birdwatching; photography; and visiting ancient village sites, petroglyphs, and totems. Unguided activities: walking, hiking, birdwatching, and photography. **Location:** In B.C., Alberta, the Yukon, and the Northwest Territories, on the Chilcotin-Fraser, Tatshenshini-Alsek, Skeena, Babine, and Firth rivers. The rivers run through Kluane, Glacier Bay, Tatshenshini-Alsek, Ivvavik, and Ts'yl-os parks. **Level of difficulty:** Gentle floating with some small and moderate whitewater rapids. Several trips consist almost entirely of gentle floating. **Time:** Between June and August. Six-, eight-, eleven-, and twelve-day trips. **Cost:** $1,675 to $3,425 per person. **Extras for additional cost:** Tents, sleeping bags, and sleeping mats for rent. **In the adventure travel operator's own words:** "Our expeditions offer a rich and rewarding natural experience. Only a few hours are spent on the rafts on travelling days, so there is time for walking and hiking to view birds, wildlife, and vistas. The trips run through some of the most remarkable parks on the continent. For over two decades, we've operated in an environmentally sensitive and sustainable manner. On each trip, expert resource people share their insights and knowledge of the area. Our skilled, knowledgeable guides are trained and licensed, so your wilderness experience is full, fun, and safe."

Section 29: Guided river rafting and river running

Kumsheen Raft Adventures

Bernie Fandrich
Highway 1
Mail: Box 30
Lytton, BC V0K 1Z0
(604) 455-2296
Fax: (604) 455-2297

Scheduled and customized guided trips: power river rafting and paddle river rafting. Guided activities on some trips: rock climbing and rappelling, mountain biking, horseback trail riding, hiking, and paintball tag games. **Location:** The Thompson and Fraser rivers, near Lytton. Three-hour, one-day, and two-day Thompson trips start at the rafting centre on Highway 1, 6 kilometres (4 miles) northeast of Lytton. Two- and three-day Thompson/Fraser trips start at the Gold Nugget Motel in Yale. **Level of difficulty:** No experience necessary. Power rafts recommended for first-time river rafters; minimum age ten. Paddle river rafting trips require swimming ability and good health; minimum age twelve. Minimum age ten to raft the Thompson River; minimum age twelve to raft the Fraser River. **Time:** Between May and October. Three-hour, one-day, two-day, and three-day trips. **Cost/what provided:** Three-hour power rafting trip: adult $72, youth (ten to sixteen years) $49. Power or paddle rafting day trip: adult $98, youth $65. Two-day Ashcroft to Lytton power or paddle rafting trip: adult $219, youth $159. Two-day Spences Bridge to Yale power rafting trip: adult $235, youth $179. Two-day Spences Bridge to Lytton (twice) power and paddle rafting trip: adult $219, youth $159. Three-day Ashcroft to Yale power rafting trip: adult $329, youth $259. Rafting trips include guide service, rafting equipment, wetsuits (paddle rafting only), rain gear, pre-trip snack, return transportation from trip's starting point to river, meals (no meal on three-hour trip), and use of rafting centre facilities. Two-day weekend combination trip: $198 per person, including two nights of camping, four meals beginning with lunch on Saturday, transportation to campsites, and all necessary equipment for activities. Group rates. Visa, MasterCard. **Extras for additional cost:** Mountain bikes, tents, sleeping bags, and mats for rent. Campsites. Barbecue. **In the adventure travel operator's own words:** "Your safety depends on our experience. Since 1973, we have safely shared an unforgettable adventure with over 100,000 guests."

Section 29:   Guided river rafting and river running

REO Rafting Adventures
Nahatlatch River Resort

612—1200 West Pender Street
Vancouver, BC V6E 2S9
(604) 684-4438
Toll free: 1-800-736-7238
Fax: (604) 684-9536

Scheduled and customized guided whitewater river rafting trips. River rafting guide training course. A resort—Nahatlatch River Resort—at starting point of trips. **Location:** Thompson, Nahatlatch, and Stein rivers. Trips begin at the resort, twenty minutes' drive off Highway 1, near Boston Bar, 200 kilometres from Vancouver. **Time:** Between April and October. One-day and multi-day trips. Fourteen-day river rafting guide training course in May. **Level of difficulty:** Beginner to experienced rafters. **What provided:** Six- to eight-person self-bailing rafts, wetsuits, wetsuit booties, instruction, guide service, mid-river snack, hot tub, sauna, beach volleyball, games area, campfire pit, showers, and washrooms. **Extras for additional cost:** Meals on a river-view dining patio. **Accommodation:** The resort has group campsites, seven cabin tents, log cabin with private bathroom, and guest house with kitchen and private bathroom. Limited electricity. **In the adventure travel operator's own words:** "The wildest whitewater in the West and an exclusive 11-acre wilderness resort that overlooks the jade-green Nahatlatch River. All our guides are trained and licensed; we provide safety instruction, equipment, helmets, and kayak escorts on all Class IV whitewater trips. Enjoy incredible rafting on some of B.C.'s best white water, and relax while we cater your vacation."

Section 29: Guided river rafting and river running

Cross-references

Iskutine Lodge—northwestern B.C.; p. 16

Blaeberry Mountain Lodge—the Rocky and Purcell mountains; p. 19

Mount Revelstoke and Glacier National Parks—Mount Revelstoke and Glacier national parks in the Columbia Mountains between Golden and Revelstoke; p. 20

Kapristo Lodge—the Rocky Mountains near Golden; p. 22

Canusa Cycle Tours—B.C.; Alberta; Montana; p. 31

Assiniboine Heli Tours/Mount Engadine Lodge—the Rocky Mountains near Banff National Park; p. 85

Nimmo Bay Heli-Ventures—northern Vancouver Island and nearby mainland areas; p. 86

Timberwolf Tours—the Rocky Mountain parks; p. 90

Jasper Adventure Centre—Jasper National Park; p. 93

Lake Louise Inn—Banff National Park and area; p. 115

The Edgewater—the Whistler area; p. 117

Section 30: Guided scuba diving

Rendezvous Dive Ventures Ltd.

Box 135
Port Alberni, BC V9Y 7M6
(604) 724-8601

Scheduled and customized guided scuba diving trips from a 36-foot customized dive boat. A waterfront lodge. **Location:** Barkley Sound on the west coast of Vancouver Island, including the Broken Islands, the Deer Group Islands, and the Chain Group Islands. Trips start at Port Alberni. **Some highlights:** Reefs covered with colourful marine life, six-gill sharks, sea lions, wolf eels, octopuses, and shipwrecks. **Level of difficulty:** Divers must be certified. **Time:** Minimum of two days. **Cost/what provided:** $135 to $150 per person per day, including meals, accommodation at the lodge, and transportation to and from dive sites. Tanks and weights on request. The dive boat is equipped with a dive safety pick-up boat, a head, a galley, a swim grid, and a boarding ladder. Group rates. **Accommodation:** The lodge has five double-occupancy guest rooms, a hot tub, a 10-cfm (cubic foot per minute) compressor, a back-up compressor, and a high-pressure air bank. **In the adventure travel operator's own words:** "Holiday at our secluded waterfront lodge and discover the underwater world of Barkley Sound on the west coast of Vancouver Island."

Section 30: Guided scuba diving

Clavella Adventures

Box 866
Nanaimo, BC V9R 5N2
(604) 753-3751
Fax: (604) 755-4014

Scheduled and customized guided scuba diving trips from a 61-foot live-aboard boat. Guided activities on some trips: underwater photography, diving with dolphins, whale watching, hot springs tours, beach hikes, kayaking, and visits to ancient Native villages. **Location**: The B.C. coast, including the Gulf Islands, Georgia Strait, Johnstone Strait, Robson Bight, Queen Charlotte Strait, the Queen Charlotte Islands, Kyuquot Sound, and Nootka Sound. **Some highlights:** Whales, dolphins, sea lions, soft corals, octopuses, and colourful fish. **Time:** Year round. Two- to ten-day trips. Three to five dives per day. **Cost/what provided:** From $119 per person per day, including divemaster service, tanks, weights, unlimited air, accommodation, meals, and snacks. Hydrophone (underwater microphone) on board. **Accommo-dation**: On board the boat, in double- and quadruple-occupancy cabins. **In the adventure travel operator's own words:** "Since 1980 we have offered full-service live-aboard diving trips on our Coast Guard certified 61-foot vessel that allow you to experience B.C.'s beautiful coast in comfort and safety. Our trips are scheduled to coincide with the arrival of whales, dolphins, and sea lions in a number of locations along the coast. We know the tides, currents, area highlights, and dive sites with the best visibility. The captain and crew will share their knowledge and experience about each area you visit. Our northern B.C. diving trips offer some of the best diving in the world, with high concentrations of soft corals, colourful fish, and invertebrates. Our specialties are trips designed for underwater photographers, marine mammal lovers, and naturalists. Join us for a trip to remember."

Section 31: Guided surfing and heli-surfing

Cross-reference

Island Sauvage Guiding Company—Vancouver Island; p. 18

Section 32: Guided sailing

Cross-references

Kermodei Wilderness Tours—the northern coast of B.C.; the Inside Passage near Kitimat; p. 23

Old Salt Charters—the Gulf Islands; the Inside Passage; the Queen Charlotte Islands; the west coast of Vancouver Island; the Caribbean; Europe; Thailand; Alaska; San Diego; Cabo San Lucas; Puerto Vallarta; Hawaii; p. 82

Hollyhock—Cortes Island in the northern Gulf Islands; p. 107

Fair Winds Sailing School—the Gulf Islands; p. 111

Section 33: Guided salmon and other saltwater fishing

Harvest Charters

Box 458
Masset, BC V0T 1M0
(604) 626-5152

Customized guided ocean and river fishing trips. **Location:** The Queen Charlotte Islands. Trips start 5 kilometres (3 miles) south of Masset. **Some highlights:** Fishing for all five species of salmon as well as halibut and groundfish. **Cost/what provided:** Ocean and river fishing trips: $300 per person per day, including guide service, eight hours of fishing in 20-foot covered boats, fishing tackle, box lunch, catch care, and cottage accommodation. **Accommodation:** Fully equipped kitchenette cottages near the beach. **More information:** Local attractions include nature reserves, bird sanctuaries, rare birds, museums, and ancient Haida villages.

Section 33: Guided salmon and other saltwater fishing

Action Adventures

Jim Hall
11146 Larson Road
Delta, BC V4C 1S5
(604) 599-0218

Scheduled and customized guided salmon fishing trips on board a 26-foot cruiser. On some trips: whale watching, wildlife viewing, and sightseeing. **Location:** The Gulf of Georgia and the Gulf Islands. Trips start in Vancouver, Steveston, and Delta. **Some highlights:** Killer whales, sea lions, ospreys, eagles, and coastal birds. **Time:** Five-hour, one-day, and overnight trips. **Cost/what provided:** Five-hour trip, $250 to $325, depending on number of participants; additional hours, $50 to $65 per hour. Overnight Gulf Islands trip, $500 to $700, depending on number of participants. Includes guide service, rods, tackle, and other fishing equipment. Overnight trips include meals and accommodation on board. Off-season and family rates. **In the adventure travel operator's own words:** "Chinook, coho, sockeye, and pink salmon are caught on 95 percent of our trips. Relax and enjoy quaint villages, secluded bays, unknown passages, and private beaches. This will be an experience of a lifetime."

Section 33: Guided salmon and other saltwater fishing

Cross-references

Kermodei Wilderness Tours—the northern coast of B.C.; the Inside Passage near Kitimat; p. 23

Geoff Evans Kayak Centre—various locations in B.C.; p. 50

Silver Fox Marine Charters—the Inside Passage from Campbell River to Bella Coola; p. 81

Nimmo Bay Heli-Ventures—northern Vancouver Island and nearby mainland areas; p. 86

Section 34: Guided freshwater fishing

Cross-references

Harvest Charters—the Queen Charlotte Islands; p. 69

Rainbow Mountain Outfitting—Tweedsmuir Park; p. 75

Bracewell's Alpine Wilderness Adventures—the Chilcotin Plateau; p. 78

Assiniboine Heli Tours/Mount Engadine Lodge—the Rocky Mountains near Banff National Park; p. 85

Section 35: Guided heli-fishing and airplane fishing

Bare Lake Resort

Terry and June Benesh
Box 1248
Kamloops, BC V2C 6H3
(604) 376-4547

Scheduled and customized guided and unguided heli-fishing trips at a fly-in trout fishing resort—Bare Lake Resort. Unguided trips and activities: hiking and photography. **Location:** Bare Lake and seven surrounding lakes north of Kamloops. The resort is 95 air kilometres (60 air miles) north of Kamloops, on Bare Lake. Return helicopter flights from Kamloops airport to the resort at no additional cost. **Some highlights:** Pine forests, meadows, bald eagles, ospreys, moose, deer, bears, and eight managed lakes for trout fishing. **Time:** Between June and September. Three-, five-, and seven-day trips. **Cost/what provided:** Three days, $750 per person; five days, $1,150 per person; seven days, $1,370 per person. Includes return helicopter flight from Kamloops airport to the resort; meals; lakeshore cabin with bedding and linen; housekeeping; 110-volt power; rowboats on all lakes; and motorboats on the larger lakes. Fish are cleaned, smoked, or kept fresh, as guests prefer. Family, group, and children's rates. **Accommodation:** Lakeshore cabins. **More information:** Fishing licences and tackle available at the resort. **In the adventure travel operator's own words:** "We hope that we will have the opportunity to serve you as one of our guests and show you a unique fishing experience."

Section 35: Guided heli-fishing and airplane fishing

Cross-references

Iskutine Lodge—northwestern B.C.; p. 16

Pemberton Helicopters—the Coast Mountains near Whistler; p. 44

Assiniboine Heli Tours/Mount Engadine Lodge—the Rocky Mountains near Banff National Park; p. 85

Nimmo Bay Heli-Ventures—northern Vancouver Island and nearby mainland areas; p. 86

The Edgewater—the Whistler area; p. 117

Section 36: Guided horseback trail riding and packhorse trips

Canadian Adventure Safaris

Natasha Aasland
2200 Kimberley Highway NE
Mail: SS3 Site 15 Box 24
Cranbrook, BC V1C 6H3
(604) 426-3566 or (604) 426-1962
Fax: (604) 426-3574

Scheduled and customized guided trips: alpine horseback riding and alpine hiking/backpacking combination. Unguided activities: nature walks, wildlife viewing, and photography. Wilderness survival camp for children. **Location:** Mountainous terrain in the White Swan area of the Rocky Mountains, 90 kilometres north of Cranbrook. Base camp elevation 1,046 metres (3,400 feet); top camp elevation 1,846 metres (6,000 feet). Return transportation from Cranbrook airport to Cranbrook and from Cranbook to mountain cabins at no additional cost. **Some highlights:** Elk, mountain goats, deer, alpine lakes, and hot springs. **Level of difficulty:** All levels. **Time:** Guided trips: three days and two nights or five days and four nights. Longer trips available. Three-day wilderness survival camp for children. **Cost/what provided:** Three days and two nights, $375 per person. Five days and four nights, $625 per person. Includes meals, accommodation, guide service, and return transportation from Cranbrook airport to Cranbrook and from Cranbrook to mountain cabins. Wilderness survival camp for children eight to twelve: $169 per child, all inclusive; parent may accompany child for $100 per day. **Extras for additional cost:** Fishing licences, purchased in advance. **Accommodation:** Base camp and top camp with sleeping cabins and cooking and dining cabins. The base camp has a sauna and shower. **In the adventure travel operator's own words:** "Explore with us on horseback the high country of the Canadian Rockies. Wildflowers, alpine meadows, and crystal-clear creeks are all features of this picturesque area. Our tours will take you through some of the most game-abundant country in the world."

Section 36: Guided horseback trail riding and packhorse trips

Big Bar Guest Ranch

Box 27, Jesmond
Clinton, BC V0K 1K0
(604) 459-2333
Fax: (604) 459-2333

A full-facility guest ranch with a guest house and self-contained log cabins—Big Bar Guest Ranch—providing scheduled and customized guided horseback riding, horse-drawn sleigh riding, and gold panning and unguided trips and activities including trout fishing, flatwater canoeing, hiking, swimming, mountain biking, and gold panning and (in winter) cross-country skiing, ice skating, and ice fishing. **Location:** Near Clinton, in the Cariboo region, adjacent to the Marble Mountain Range. Return transportation from the B.C. Rail station and the Greyhound bus depot at Clinton to the guest ranch at an additional cost. **Level of difficulty:** Stamina and a good level of physical fitness required for horseback riding. Weight limitations. **Time:** Guided overnight pack trips, from one night to several days. Guided horseback riding day trips. Customized trips: call for information. **Cost/what provided:** Guided overnight pack trips for six days and five nights: $699 to $741 per adult, $515 per child aged eight to fourteen. Includes meals, first and last nights' accommodation at the ranch, horses, tack, tents, foam to sleep on, and guide service. Guided horseback riding, two-hour to full-day rides: $26 to $62 per person. **Extras for additional cost:** Recreational vehicle hook-ups. Boarding for guests' own horses. Sleigh rides. **Accommodation:** The twelve-room full-service guest house: $65 to $104 per room, including three meals per day. Self-contained log cabins: $75 to $110 per cabin; meals available at $36 per day. The guest ranch has a hot tub, a billiard room, a lounge, and a video room. Dining room and guest rooms are smoke-free. Children's rates available for guest house and cabins. Tents are used on pack trips. **More information:** Pets welcome. **In the adventure travel operator's own words:** "Discover ranching and leave the chores to us. Leave fast-paced clatter behind and get in touch with some old-fashioned sensations—the call of an owl, the yip yip of coyotes, the sight of unbelievably clear skies, the swift rush of horses before they're gathered for saddling. You will make new friends and feel like a special family guest—that's the type of place you're visiting."

Section 36: Guided horseback trail riding and packhorse trips

Rainbow Mountain Outfitting

David Dorsey, Jr.
Box 3066
Anahim Lake, BC V0L 1C0
(604) 742-3539
Fax: (604) 742-3411

Scheduled and customized guided trips: alpine horseback riding, hiking with horses carrying gear, and freshwater fishing pack trips. **Location:** Tweedsmuir Park, in the Rainbow Mountains of west central B.C. Fishing trips follow the Mackenzie Grease Trail, with fishing in the rivers and lakes of the Dean and Blackwater watersheds. **Level of difficulty:** Horseback riding and hiking of moderate difficulty, with an average of 17 kilometres between camps. **Time:** Between July and mid-September. Six- to ten-day trips. **Cost/what provided:** Six- to ten-day trips, $1,195 to $1,395 per person. Includes all equipment and guide service. Personal belongings and equipment transported by pack horses. **Extras for additional cost:** Float plane on some trips. **In the adventure travel operator's own words:** "We bring generations of tradition, knowledge, and experience to a true wilderness adventure. Ride, camp, hike, fish, and explore with us the colourful mountains, lush valleys, and historic Mackenzie Grease Trail of the Chilcotin Plateau."

Section 36: Guided horseback trail riding and packhorse trips

Pemberton Stables

Don Menzel
Box 7
Pemberton, BC V0N 2L0
(604) 894-6615

Scheduled and customized guided horseback trail riding trips. **Location:** The Pemberton Valley, near Whistler. **Some highlights:** 300-metre (1,000-foot) climb on horseback to view the Pemberton Valley. **Time:** Two-hour, one-day, and two-day trips. **Cost/what provided:** Two-hour ride, $35 per person. Day ride, $100 per person. Two-day ride, $200 per person, including meals, guide service, and tents. **Extras for additional cost:** Return van transportation from Whistler, $10 to $30 per person, depending on van occupancy. Steak barbecue on day ride, $15 per person. **In the adventure travel operator's own words:** "Our trail rides leave from the ranch, cross open fields, and climb 1,000 feet onto a hillside that offers a terrific view of the Pemberton Valley. Our combination of friendly horses and magnificent scenery will make your ride unforgettable."

Section 36: Guided horseback trail riding and packhorse trips

Quilchena Hotel and Resort

Jill Rose
General Delivery
Quilchena, BC V0E 2R0
(604) 378-2611
Fax: (604) 378-6091

A ranch resort—Quilchena Hotel and Resort—providing scheduled and customized guided trail rides on horseback and unguided trips and activities, including golf, hiking, birdwatching, mountain biking, swimming, tennis, freshwater fishing, and windsurfing. Barbecues and hay rides. Recreational vehicle park. Marina. **Location:** Quilchena, near Nicola Lake, between Merritt and Kamloops. **Accommodation and other facilities:** Full-facility ranch house, $97 per room, based on double occupancy; additional $8.50 per person to a maximum of six people. Sixteen-room hotel, shared bathrooms, $64 to $74 per room, based on double occupancy. Recreational vehicle park. Banquet facilities available. **In the adventure travel operator's own words:** "Ambience, Gemütlichkeit—call it what you will. Ours is a blend of local ranch flavour, elegant historical surroundings, contemporary attitude, and old-fashioned friendliness. Fine dining is our specialty. Come and experience one of B.C.'s largest working cattle ranches."

Section 36: Guided horseback trail riding and packhorse trips

Bracewell's Alpine Wilderness Adventures

Alex and Connie Bracewell
Box 1
Tatlayoko Lake, BC V0L 1W0
Phone and fax: (604) 476-1169

Scheduled and customized guided trips and other activities from a ranch—the Circle X Ranch. Guided trips: pack trips on horseback, trail rides on horseback, freshwater fishing, fishing tours by vehicle, wildlife viewing, hiking, heli-hiking, helicopter and airplane sightseeing flights, alpine ski touring, glacier tours, prospecting, and area history tours. Each guided pack trip on horseback focuses on one or more of the following: wilderness photography, wildlife viewing, fishing, Native and pioneer skills, outdoor survival training skills, glacier tours, and prospecting. Other activities: riding lessons; seasonal ranch activities including haying, breaking horses, and gymkhana horse sports; birdwatching; swimming; canoeing; and cross-country skiing. **Location:** On the Chilcotin Plateau, 260 air kilometres (160 air miles) north of Vancouver. A four-hour drive from Williams Lake. There is a 4,000-foot gravel airstrip on the ranch. The ranch is on 160 acres of wilderness. **Some highlights:** Alpine wildflower meadows, glacier-fed lakes, mule deer, grizzly and black bears, mountain goats, bald eagles, and other birds. **Level of difficulty:** All ages and abilities. **Time:** The ranch is open between February and August and is open Christmas and New Year's by arrangement. Eight-day pack trips in July and August. Five-day pack trips between May and August. Fishing tour by vehicle between May and August. Wildlife viewing in June. Alpine ski touring in February and March. Other trips and activities: call for information. **Cost/what provided:** Eight-day pack trip, $1,055 per person; five-day pack trip, $825 per person. Pack trips include guide service, horses; meals; mountain cabin or mountain camps, depending on weather and location; and one night's accommodation at the log ranch house before and after each trip. Fishing trip, $660 per person. Wildlife viewing trip, $660 per person. Other guided trips: call for rates. Seniors' and children's rates. **Accommodation:** Mountain cabin, mountain camps, and teepees on trips. Accommodation at the ranch in a full-facility log ranch house, $55 to $65, depending on occupancy. Meals $35 per day, children under thirteen half rate. **Group size:** Maximum of ten people on each trip. **In the adventure travel operator's own words:** "Successfully view unsuspecting wildlife amidst mountain meadows and fragile alpine flowers. Explore fifty-million-year-old fossil outcrops and discover local and Native history. Return to our ten-thousand-square-foot log ranch house with full amenities to relax and enjoy the day's memories. We have four generations of experience at combining the Chilcotin's best natural, physical, and cultural resources. We have created packages that will satisfy your expectations for excitement and adventure."

Section 36: Guided horseback trail riding and packhorse trips

T Bar T Total Wilderness Experience

Thomas Hillman
RR 2
Quesnel, BC V2J 3H6
(604) 747-8620

Scheduled and customized guided pack trips on horseback. **Location:** The Baezaeko River Valley, in the Itcha Mountains, in the Cariboo area. **Time:** Ten-day pack trips. **What provided:** Guide service, horses and rigging, meals, tents, sleeping gear, and all-weather outerwear. **In the adventure travel operator's own words:** "An experience for the true outdoor enthusiast. Bring a lust for high country adventure."

Section 36: Guided horseback trail riding and packhorse trips

Cross-references

Section 37: Guided all-terrain vehicle trips

Bearhead Creek Wilderness Tours

Barry Himer
Box 1051
Falher, AB T0H 1M0
(403) 837-8263

Scheduled and customized guided trips and activities from a lodge and cabins—Bearhead Creek Lodge. Guided trips and activities: all-terrain vehicle trail riding, snowmobiling, hiking, wildlife viewing, birdwatching, and nature photography. **Location:** The Peace River area. Trips begin at the lodge, 60 kilometres southeast of the town of Peace River, near Highway 2. The lodge is on 160 acres of forests and meadowlands. **Time:** Between May and October; open in winter by arrangement. **Cost/what provided:** Day trips: $100 per person, $150 per family (two adults, two children under twelve years), including meals, overnight accommodation, and guide service. Weekend trips: $200 per person, $300 per family (two adults, two children under twelve years) including meals, accommodation, and guide service. **Extras for additional cost:** All-terrain vehicle rental. **Accommodation:** The lodge is 1,000 square feet in size and has a kitchen/dining room area, a bathroom, and a sleeping area. There are three guest cabins. **In the adventure travel operator's own words:** "Come and enjoy our quiet, peaceful wilderness retreat."

Section 38: Guided boat cruises and boat tours

Silver Fox Marine Charters

Ian Andersen
Quarterdeck Marina
Port Hardy, BC
Mail: 1653 Beaconsfield Court
Comox, BC V9M 1A9
Toll-free in B.C.: (604) 978-9069

Scheduled and customized guided nature-oriented cruises and fishing trips for five salmon species (in season), halibut, lingcod, and rockfish. **Location:** Along the Inside Passage from Campbell River to Bella Coola. **Some highlights:** Bald eagles, black-tailed deer, grizzly and black bears, orcas, minke whales, porpoises, seals, sea lions, and many species of coastal birds. **Time:** Four-day cruises in July and August; longer cruises if booked far enough in advance. Customized cruises in May and in June and in September and October. **Cost/what provided:** Four-day cruises: $680 per person, based on four people sharing; includes meals, non-alcoholic drinks, Zodiac inflatable with outboard, guide service, fishing tackle, and rain gear. Customized cruises: from $150 per person. **Accommodation:** On board 40-foot boat, maximum six people (three double beds). Full cooking and freezing facilities, toilet, hot shower, 110-volt power, TV, VCR, and radio telephone. Wheelchair accessible—large rear deck and level access throughout the interior. First and last nights' accommodation at a hotel in Port Hardy.

Section 38: Guided boat cruises and boat tours

Old Salt Charters Ltd.

Barry G. Buckle
2086 West Seventh Avenue
Vancouver, BC V6J 1T4
(604) 736-0238
Fax: (604) 736-0248

Customized skippered and bare boat sailboat and powerboat charters for large and small groups. Offshore/coastal sail and learn trips. **Location:** Customized trips: the Gulf Islands; the Inside Passage; Glacier Bay, Alaska; the Queen Charlotte Islands; the west coast of Vancouver Island; the Caribbean; Europe; and Thailand. Offshore/coastal sail and learn trips: to San Diego, Cabo San Lucas, Puerto Vallarta, and Hawaii, on a 42-foot sailing vessel; maximum four people per boat. **In the adventure travel operator's own words:** "We offer the most versatile charter opportunities in the Pacific Northwest: sail or power, leisure or adventure, coastal or offshore, we can help you."

Section 38: Guided boat cruises and boat tours

Nature Connection

Box 634
Nanaimo, BC V9R 5N2
(604) 753-3751
Fax: (604) 755-4014

Scheduled and customized guided nature-oriented and whale watching trips on board a 61-foot live-aboard boat. Guided activities on some trips: rainforest hiking, photography, wildlife viewing, hot springs tours, sea kayaking, and visiting ancient Native villages. **Location:** The B.C. coast. Nature-oriented trips: South Moresby Park in the Queen Charlotte Islands. Trips begin at Sandspit Airport and Queen Charlotte City. Nature-oriented trips include visits to Dolomite Narrows, Windy Bay, the Copper Islands, and ancient Haida villages including Kloo (Tanu), Quna (Skedans), and Sgan Gwaii (Anthony Island). Whale watching trips: Johnstone Strait, Robson Bight, and the Inside Passage of B.C. Trips begin in Port Hardy on northern Vancouver Island. Whale watching trips include visits to whale and dolphin research sites including Paul Spong's Orcalab and to historic village sites. **Time:** Between June and September. Two- to ten-day trips. **Cost/what provided:** From $159 per person per day. Includes guide service, accommodation, meals, and snacks. Hydrophone (underwater microphone) on board. Group rates. **Accommodation:** On board the boat, in double- and quadruple-occupancy cabins. **In the adventure travel operator's own words:** "The islands, waters, and natural history of Gwaii Haanas (South Moresby) and the northern Inside Passage provide a remarkable backdrop for exploring, learning about, and photographing the lands, forests, culture, and biological diversity of these unique areas. Some of the richest and most spectacular ecosystems that exist on our planet are here. Our photography and naturalist tours have provided access to these undeveloped, remote areas since 1980. B.C. is home to the highest concentration of killer whales in the world; we know where the whales are and how they behave, and we will put you in the best position to capture spectacular images."

Section 38: Guided boat cruises and boat tours

Cross-references

Kapristo Lodge—the Rocky Mountains near Golden; p. 22

Kermodei Wilderness Tours—the northern coast of B.C.; the Inside Passage near Kitimat; p. 23

Action Adventures—the Gulf of Georgia; the Gulf Islands; p. 70

Nimmo Bay Heli-Ventures—northern Vancouver Island and nearby mainland areas; p. 86

Fair Winds Sailing School—the Gulf Islands; p. 111

Section 39: Guided heli-sightseeing and airplane sightseeing

Cross-references

Iskutine Lodge—northwestern B.C.; p. 16

Bracewell's Alpine Wilderness Adventures—the Chilcotin Plateau; p. 78

Nimmo Bay Heli-Ventures—northern Vancouver Island and nearby mainland areas; p. 86

Canadian River Expeditions—B.C.; Alberta; the Yukon; the Northwest Territories; p. 91

Cave Treks—Vancouver Island; p. 102

Lake Louise Inn—Banff National Park and area; p. 115

The Edgewater—the Whistler area; p. 117

Section 40: Guided heli-adventures and airplane adventures

Assiniboine Heli Tours Inc.
Mount Engadine Lodge

Jackie Cheng
Box 2430
Canmore, AB T0L 0M0
(403) 678-5459
Fax: (403) 678-3075

Scheduled and customized guided trips from a backcountry mountain lodge—Mount Engadine Lodge—and from other locations in Alberta and B.C. Trips from the lodge include one or more of the following activities: heli-hiking, heli-fishing, heli–glacier tours, hiking, horseback trail rides, river rafting, and freshwater fishing. Trips from other locations include ranch holidays with horseback trail rides, river rafting, and freshwater fishing and heli-skiing. **Location:** Trips from the lodge: in the Banff National Park area, in the Rocky Mountains. The lodge is 38 kilometres south of Canmore, in the Kananaskis area. Canmore is at the eastern entrance of Banff National Park. Trips from other locations: ranch holidays just east of the Banff National Park area; heli-skiing in the Rocky Mountains and the Chilcotin area of B.C. **Some highlights:** Alpine walks and picnics by secluded lakes, miles of paths, towering peaks, wildlife, and birds. **Level of difficulty:** All ages and abilities. **Cost/what provided:** Rates include guide service, accomodation, meals, and afternoon tea with homemade cakes. **Accommodation:** Lodge rooms and cabin rooms. The lodge has fireplaces, a sauna, and an outdoor Jacuzzi. **In the adventure travel operator's own words:** "May your spirit soar. Join us for a taste of adventure with a taste of home."

Section 40: Guided heli-adventures and airplane adventures

Nimmo Bay Heli-Ventures

Craig Murray
Box 696
Port McNeill, BC V0N 2R0
(604) 956-4000
Fax: (604) 956-2000

Scheduled and customized guided trips from a resort—Nimmo Bay Resort—accessible only by helicopter. Guided trips: heli-adventures, heli-fishing, heli-fishing/coastal nature cruises combination, heli-fishing/saltwater fishing combination, heli-sightseeing, sea kayaking, and river kayaking. Other guided activities on some trips: river float trips, whale watching, caving, and wildlife viewing. **Location:** Northern Vancouver Island area (including the west coast of Vancouver Island) and nearby mainland areas, including Kingcome Inlet and Nimmo Bay. Trips start at the resort, in Nimmo Bay. Helicopter and float plane transportation from Port Hardy on northern Vancouver Island to the resort at an additional cost. Port Hardy is a one-hour flight or an eight-hour drive, including ferry trip, from Vancouver. **Level of difficulty:** For many levels of fitness and skill. Seniors and physically challenged people are welcome. **Time:** Heli-adventures between May and October. Heli-fishing between April and October. Saltwater fishing between July 15 and October 30. Sea kayaking between May and October. **Cost/what provided:** Heli-adventure: three days $3,895 per person, four days $5,175 per person; includes helicopter service, food, guided sightseeing, wildlife viewing, and whale watching. Heli-fishing: three days $3,895 per person, four days $5,175 per person; includes helicopter

Section 40: Guided heli-adventures and airplane adventures

service, guide service, food, fishing gear, all-weather gear, and accommodation at the resort; spin and fly fishing instruction available. Heli-fishing/nature cruise combination: four days $3,895 per person; includes helicopter service, guide service, 24-foot vessel, food, fishing gear, all-weather gear, and accommodation at the resort. Heli-fishing/saltwater fishing combination: four days $3,895 per person; includes helicopter service, food, two days of heli-fishing, two days of saltwater fishing, guide service, fishing gear, all-weather gear, two days' accommodation at the resort, and two days' accommodation at Ocean Salmon Lodge. Sea kayaking and river float trip: four days $3,895 per person; includes one day of heli-fishing, one day of heli-adventure, one or two days of sea kayaking, one-day river float trip, helicopter service, fishing gear, food, transportation, and accommodation at the resort. Sea and river kayaking: four days $3,495 per person; includes helicopter service, guide service, kayaks, food, and accommodation at the resort. Visa, cheques. **Extras for additional cost:** Flights from Vancouver and Port Hardy to Nimmo Bay Resort. Fishing licences can be bought at Nimmo Bay. **Accommodation:** The resort accommodates twelve guests. Rates include access to telephone and fax, audio-visual centre, satellite TV, billiards room, and waterfall hot tub. **In the adventure travel operator's own words:** "We would like you to participate in one of life's truly great adventures—one that you cannot possibly imagine and that will put you in touch with the heart of the true wilderness environment."

Section 40: Guided heli-adventures and airplane adventures

Cross-references

Purcell Lodge/ABC Wilderness Adventures—the Purcell Mountains near Golden on the east boundary of Glacier National Park; p. 12

Cave Treks—Vancouver Island; p. 102

Section 41: Guided hot air balloon rides

Balloons Above the Valley

110—19329 Enterprise Way
Surrey, BC V3S 6J8
(604) 533-2378
Evenings: (604) 657-4908 or (604) 649-4167
For reservations: 1-800-465-2378
Fax: (604) 534-7966

Scheduled and customized guided hot air balloon trips. **Location:** In the Fraser Valley, starting in Langley, and in the Nicola Valley, starting in Merritt. For the Merritt trip, return van transportation from Langley to Merritt at no additional cost. **Level of difficulty:** All ages and abilities. **Time:** The Fraser Valley trip, one hour to one and one-half hours, between May and October. The Nicola Valley trip, one day, including return transportation time from Langley to Merritt, between November and April. **Cost/what provided:** The Fraser Valley trip, $99 to $175 per person, including guide service and champagne after trip. The Nicola Valley trip, $180 to $250 per person, including guide service, hot cider, lunch at the Coldwater Hotel in Merritt, and return van transportation from Langley to Merritt. Group rates. Visa, MasterCard. **In the adventure travel operator's own words:** "The memories of your flight will last a lifetime. On our Fraser Valley trip, our hot air balloon, the *Flying Eagle*, will carry you over one of the most magnificent and fertile valleys on earth. After your flight, balloon pins and a frameable flight certificate will be presented as mementos of your time with us."

Section 41: Guided hot air balloon rides

Cross-reference

Canusa Cycle Tours—B.C.; Alberta; Montana; p. 31

Section 42: Guided nature expeditions

Timberwolf Tours Ltd.
**Other trips offered by this adventure
travel operator, page 41.**

**13 Menlo Crescent
Sherwood Park, AB T8A 0R8
(403) 467-9697
Fax: (403) 467-7686**

Scheduled and customized guided trips: camping trips and hotel-to-hotel trips with guided activities including mountain biking, river rafting, hiking, and wilderness canoeing; hiking; packhorse trips/guest ranch holidays; and wilderness canoeing with pre-trip instruction. **Location:** Most trips begin in Calgary and include the Rocky Mountain parks. Hiking in the Kananaskis area and in Banff, Jasper, and Yoho national parks. Packhorse trips/guest ranch holidays in the eastern Rocky Mountains near Rocky Mountain House. Wilderness canoe trips on the Athabasca River system—the Athabasca, Wildhay, and Berland rivers—start in Edmonton or near Jasper. **Level of difficulty:** Participants should be in reasonably good shape. Beginners welcome. **Time:** Scheduled six- to fifteen-day camping trips between June and October. Fifteen-day hotel-to-hotel trips. Seven-day canoe trips between June and September. Other trips: call for information. **Cost/what provided:** Camping trips, $760 to $1,770 per person. Hotel-to-hotel trips, $2,745 per person. Canoe trips, $795 per person. Includes guide service, accommodation, meals, and equipment. Guides speak English, French, and German. Other trips: call for rates. Visa, MasterCard. **Group size:** Maximum of twelve people on each trip. **Accommodation:** Hotels, bed and breakfasts, cabins, and/or tents, depending on trip. **In the adventure travel operator's own words:** "We take pride in our level of service and safety. From your first contact with us to your last farewell, we strive to make you comfortable and your holiday a safe and enjoyable experience."

Section 42: Guided nature expeditions

Vancouver Natural History Society
Other trips offered by this adventure travel operator,
pages 110 and 112.

Box 3021, Main Post Office
Vancouver, BC V6B 3X5
(604) 525-9498
Fax: (604) 527-5095

Scheduled and customized guided field trips with naturalists, with an emphasis on birdwatching and the natural history of a particular area. **Location:** Various locations, from city parks to wilderness areas. **Time:** One day to one week. **More information:** Children are especially welcome on shorter trips. Family-oriented outings are also scheduled each season.

Canadian River Expeditions
22—1212 Alpha Lake Road
Mail: Box 1023
Whistler, BC V0N 1B0
Toll-free: 1-800-898-7238
Fax: (604) 938-6621

Scheduled and customized guided river rafting trips with other guided activities on some trips including airplane sightseeing; wildlife viewing; walking; hiking; birdwatching; photography; and visiting ancient village sites, petroglyphs, and totems. Unguided activities: walking, hiking, birdwatching, and photography. **Location:** In B.C., Alberta, the Yukon, and the Northwest Territories, on the Chilcotin-Fraser, Tatshenshini-Alsek, Skeena, Babine, and Firth rivers. The rivers run through Kluane, Glacier Bay, Tatshenshini-Alsek, Ivvavik, and Ts'yl-os parks. **Level of difficulty:** Gentle floating with some small and moderate whitewater rapids. Several trips consist almost entirely of gentle floating. **Time:** Between June and August. Six-, eight-, eleven-, and twelve-day trips. **Cost:** $1,675 to $3,425 per person. **Extras for additional cost:** Tents, sleeping bags, and sleeping mats for rent. **In the adventure travel operator's own words:** "Our expeditions offer a rich and rewarding natural experience. Only a few hours are spent on the rafts on travelling days, so there is time for walking and hiking to view birds, wildlife, and vistas. The trips run through some of the most remarkable parks on the continent. For over two decades, we've operated in an environmentally sensitive and sustainable manner. On each trip, expert resource people share their insights and knowledge of the area. Our skilled, knowledgeable guides are trained and licensed so your wilderness experience is full, fun, and safe."

Section 42: Guided nature expeditions

Cross-references

Purcell Lodge/ABC Wilderness Adventures—the Purcell Mountains near Golden on the east boundary of Glacier National Park; p. 12

Mount Revelstoke and Glacier National Parks—Mount Revelstoke and Glacier national parks in the Columbia Mountains between Golden and Revelstoke; p. 20

Nature Connection—the Queen Charlotte Islands; p. 83

The Edgewater—the Whistler area; p. 117

Section 43: Guided ski-lift nature tours

Cross-reference

The Edgewater—the Whistler area; p. 117

Section 44: Guided glacier tours

Jasper Adventure Centre Ltd.

Murray Morgan
625 Patricia Street
Mail: Box 1064
Jasper, AB T0E 1E0
Phone and fax: (403) 852-5595
Toll-free in Western Canada: 1-800-565-7547

Scheduled and customized guided trips in summer: glacier tours, hot springs tours, walking, and wildlife viewing. Scheduled and customized guided trips in winter: walking, ice walks, and sightseeing van tours. Information and reservations for other guided trips: whitewater rafting; horseback riding; and wilderness, whitewater, and flatwater canoeing. Information and reservations for sightseeing coach tours, ski and snowboard rentals, and accommodation. **Location:** Jasper National Park. **Some highlights:** On hot springs and wildlife viewing trips: bighorn sheep, bull elk, mountain goats, deer, bears, beavers, moose, and loons. **Level of difficulty:** All fitness levels. **Time:** Year round. Three-hour to six-and-one-half-hour trips. **Cost/what provided:** Three-hour Mount Edith Cavell tour: adult $30, child $15. Three-hour Maligne Canyon walking trip: adult $30, child $15. Four-hour Miette Hot Springs wildlife viewing trip: adult $30, child $15. Five-and-one-half-hour Columbia Icefield glacier tour: adult $60, child $30. Three-hour Maligne Valley walking and wildlife viewing trip: adult $30, child $15. Three-hour Jasper sightseeing van tour: adult $30, child $15. Six-and-one-half hour Icefields Parkway to Banff van tour: $65 one way from Jasper, $90 return. No charge for children under six on some trips. **Extras for additional cost:** Hot springs pool admission. Snocoach transportation fee on Columbia Icefield glacier tour. **In the adventure travel operator's own words:** "Our staff are certified park guides. We are your key to Jasper. Join us to experience the most scenic and fascinating areas of Jasper National Park."

Section 44: Guided glacier tours

Cross-references

Northern Lights Alpine Recreation—the Rocky and Purcell mountains near Invermere in southeastern B.C.; p. 29

Bracewell's Alpine Wilderness Adventures—the Chilcotin Plateau; p. 78

The Edgewater—the Whistler area; p. 117

Section 45: Guided heli–glacier tours and airplane glacier tours

Cross-references

Assiniboine Heli Tours/Mount Engadine Lodge—the Rocky Mountains near Banff National Park; p. 85

The Edgewater—the Whistler area; p. 117

Section 46: Guided whale watching

Stubbs Island Charters Ltd.

Bill and Donna Mackay and Jim Borrowman
Box 7
Telegraph Cove, BC V0N 3J0
(604) 928-3185 or 928-3117
Toll-free in North America for reservations: 1-800-665-3066
Fax: (604) 928-3102

Scheduled and customized guided whale watching trips aboard 60-foot vessels. **Location:** Johnstone Strait area. Trips depart from the village of Telegraph Cove on northern Vancouver Island. Telegraph Cove is one-half hour's drive south of Port McNeill and is two and one-half hours' drive north of Campbell River. **Some highlights:** Underwater microphones (hydrophones) on vessels for listening to the whales. **Level of difficulty:** All ages and fitness levels—no physical exertion required. **Time:** Between mid-June and mid-October, day trips start each day at 9:00 a.m. and finish between 1:00 and 2:00 p.m. During peak season, a second trip starts at 3:00 p.m. and finishes between 7:00 and 8:00 p.m. Check-in time for reservations is at least one-half hour before sailing time at the office, at the end of the boardwalk in Telegraph Cove in building #24. **Cost:** Adult $60, senior $54, child one to twelve $54. Visa, MasterCard. **Extras for additional cost:** Meals on board the vessels. **Accommodation:** Limited cabin accommodation is available in Telegraph Cove. Hotels and bed and breakfasts in Port McNeill, Port Hardy, and Campbell River. **In the adventure travel operator's own words:** "Our company has been whale watching since 1980 and has been involved with the research community since that time. We were the first company in B.C. to institute killer whale watching tours, and we take pride in setting the standard for responsible wildlife viewing. We have been instrumental in the planning and implementation of whale watching guidelines for this area and in the establishment of the Robson Bight (Michael Bigg) Ecological Reserve, set up especially for killer whales. Our 60-foot vessels are Coast Guard certified."

Section 46: Guided whale watching

Seasmoke Tours

Box 483
Alert Bay, BC V0N 1A0
(604) 974-5225
Toll-free in B.C.: 1-800-668-ORCA (6722)
Fax: (604) 974-2266

Scheduled and customized guided whale watching trips on board a 44-foot sailboat, a 24-foot Zodiac rigid hull inflatable raft, and a 33-foot custom-designed open boat. **Location:** Northern Vancouver Island. Trips start from Alert Bay, Alder Bay campsite near Port McNeill, and Port Hardy. **Some highlights:** Orcas (killer whales), minke whales, harbour seals, Dall's porpoises, Pacific white-sided dolphins, gray whales, humpback whales, and bald eagles. **Level of difficulty:** Sailboat: not recommended for children under three. Zodiac: not recommended for children under five, pregnant women, or people in frail health. Open boat: not recommended for children under four. **Time:** Five- to six-hour sailboat trips. Three-hour Zodiac trips. Three- to four-hour open boat trips. **Cost/what provided:** Sailboat trips: adult $65, child $55; includes guide service, meals, exposure clothing, and hydrophones. Zodiac and open boat trips: adults $55, child $50; includes guide service, exposure clothing, and hydrophones. Visa, MasterCard. **In the adventure travel operator's own words:** "Feel the heartbeat of mother nature in a safe and meaningful way with our experienced, informative skippers, who are in communication with researchers, giving you a most memorable adventure-filled experience."

Section 46: Guided whale watching

Subtidal Adventures

1950 Peninsula Road
Mail: Box 78
Ucluelet, BC V0R 3A0
Phone and fax: (604) 726-7336

Scheduled and customized guided whale watching trips on board a 36-foot former Coast Guard rescue boat and a 24-foot Zodiac rigid hull inflatable. **Location:** The west coast of Vancouver Island, in the Broken Islands Group of Pacific Rim National Park. **Some highlights:** Gray whales, humpback whales, killer whales, seals, sea lions, and eagles. **Level of difficulty:** Day trips aboard the 36-foot boat are suitable for all ages and fitness levels. Day trips aboard the Zodiac are not recommended for people with back problems or heart conditions or for pregnant women. **Time:** Year round. Gray whale spring migration in March and April. Two-, three-, and four-hour day trips. **Cost/what provided:** Adult $40 to $60, child $10 to $40. Visa, MasterCard, American Express. **In the adventure travel operator's own words:** "Experience the beauty of this island wilderness on our leisurely and relaxing afternoon boat trip or on our faster-paced morning Zodiac trip. In spring, witness part of the longest migration of any animal as over twenty thousand gray whales pass by Ucluelet on their way north to Alaska."

Section 46: Guided whale watching

Cross-references

Island Sauvage Guiding Company—Vancouver Island; p. 18

Kermodei Wilderness Tours—the northern coast of B.C.; the Inside Passage near Kitimat; p. 23

Geoff Evans Kayak Centre—various locations in B.C.; p. 50

Northern Lights Expeditions—northern Vancouver Island; p. 53

Island Sauvage Guiding Company—the Robson Bight area on northern Vancouver Island; p. 55

Clavella Adventures—the B.C. coast; p. 67

Action Adventures—the Gulf Islands; p. 70

Nature Connection—Johnstone Strait; Robson Bight; the Inside Passage of B.C.; p. 83

Nimmo Bay Heli-Ventures—northern Vancouver Island and nearby mainland areas; p. 86

Section 47: Guided wildlife viewing

Take-A-Hike Tours

Tony Harris
Box 372
Telkwa, BC V0J 2X0
Phone and fax: (604) 846-5599

Scheduled and customized guided trips: wildlife viewing, hiking, mountain biking, and cross-country and downhill skiing. Mountain bike and ski equipment rentals. **Location:** The Bulkley Valley, in the Coast Mountains. Trips start from Smithers, midway between Prince Rupert and Prince George, on Highway 16. **Some highlights:** Grizzly bears, black bears, moose, deer, caribou, beavers, otters, and bald eagles. **Level of difficulty:** All ages and fitness levels. Novice to low intermediate cross-country skiing. **Time:** One to five days. **Cost/what provided:** Day trip: from $165 per person, all inclusive. Cost varies with duration and location of trips. Includes guide service and the use of binoculars and spotting scopes for wildlife viewing. Guides speak English, French, German, and Japanese. **Group size:** Two to six guests per trip. **Extras for additional cost:** Mountain bikes and ski equipment for rent. **Accommodation:** Hotels, tents, and/or log cabin, depending on trip. **In the adventure travel operator's own words:** "We are a licensed operator for B.C. Parks in the Babine Mountain Recreation Area. We employ only professional guides with a strong interest in wildlife conservation and low-impact use of the mountain environment. We are able to offer superior wildlife viewing opportunities from a safe distance, combining guide experience with top quality binoculars and spotting scopes."

Section 47: Guided wildlife viewing

Cross-references

Purcell Lodge/ABC Wilderness Adventures—the Purcell Mountains near Golden on the east boundary of Glacier National Park; p. 12

Iskutine Lodge—northwestern B.C.; p. 16

Cathedral Lakes Lodge—the Cascade Mountains in Cathedral Park between Manning Park and Penticton; p. 21

Kermodei Wilderness Tours—the northern coast of B.C.; the Inside Passage near Kitimat; p. 23

Canusa Cycle Tours—B.C.; Alberta; Montana; p. 31

Timberwolf Tours—the Rocky Mountains; northern Alberta; the Kootenays; p. 41

Geoff Evans Kayak Centre—various locations in B.C.; p. 50

Northern Lights Expeditions—northern Vancouver Island; p. 53

Action Adventures—the Gulf of Georgia; the Gulf Islands; p. 70

Bracewell's Alpine Wilderness Adventures—the Chilcotin Plateau; p. 78

Bearhead Creek Wilderness Tours—the Peace River area; p. 80

Nature Connection—the Queen Charlotte Islands; the Inside Passage of B.C.; Johnstone Strait; Robson Bight; p. 83

Nimmo Bay Heli-Ventures—northern Vancouver Island and nearby mainland areas; p. 86

Canadian River Expeditions—B.C.; Alberta; the Yukon; the Northwest Territories; p. 91

Jasper Adventure Centre—Jasper National Park; p. 93

Section 48: Guided birdwatching

Cross-references

Purcell Lodge/ABC Wilderness Adventures—the Purcell Mountains near Golden on the east boundary of Glacier National Park; p. 12

Iskutine Lodge—northwestern B.C.; p. 16

Kapristo Lodge—the Rocky Mountains near Golden; p. 22

Bearhead Creek Wilderness Tours—the Peace River area; p. 80

Vancouver Natural History Society—various locations; p. 91

Canadian River Expeditions—B.C.; Alberta; the Yukon; the Northwest Territories; p. 91

Section 49: Guided photography

Iskutine Lodge

Box 39
Iskut, BC V0J 1K0
(604) 234-3456

Scheduled and customized guided trips and unguided activities from a lodge with cabins—Iskutine Lodge. Guided trips: wildlife photography; wildlife viewing; bird-watching; wilderness, whitewater, and flatwater canoeing and kayaking; river running; mountain biking; hiking; airplane hiking; airplane fishing; airplane sightseeing; horseback trail riding; packhorse trips; snowshoeing; cross-country skiing; and hot springs tours. Unguided activities: wind surfing, freshwater fishing, and fly fishing. **Location:** In northwestern B.C. The lodge, surrounded by over 3.5 million acres of designated wilderness (Spatsizi and Mount Edziza parks), is 100 kilometres south of Dease Lake via the Stewart--Cassiar highway, on Lake Eddontenajon, and is reached by plane, train, car, or ferry. **Some highlights:** Volcanoes and wildlife. **Level of difficulty:** Participants should be reasonably fit and active. **Time:** The lodge is open year round. Scheduled trips between June and September. Customized trips: call for details. **Cost/what provided:** $150 to $200 per person per day, all inclusive. Includes cabin and use of lodge facilities immediately before and after each trip. **Accommodation:** In the lodge and cabins. **In the adventure travel operator's own words:** "Small group size, excellent gear for many types of activities, true wilderness setting, uncompromising conservation standards, state-of-the-art nutrition, and devoted guides mean incomparable value."

Section 49: Guided photography

Cross-references

Purcell Lodge/ABC Wilderness Adventures—the Purcell Mountains near Golden on the east boundary of Glacier National Park; p. 12

Kapristo Lodge—the Rocky Mountains near Golden; p. 22

Bracewell's Alpine Wilderness Adventures—the Chilcotin Plateau; p. 78

Bearhead Creek Wilderness Tours—the Peace River area; p. 80

Nature Connection—the Queen Charlotte Islands; the Inside Passage of B.C.; Johnstone Strait; Robson Bight; p. 83

Canadian River Expeditions—B.C.; Alberta; the Yukon; the Northwest Territories; p. 91

Section 50: Guided caving and heli-caving

Cave Treks

Karen Griffiths
Box 897
Gold River, BC V0P 1G0
(604) 283-7144 or (604) 283-2283
Fax: (604) 283-2481

Scheduled and customized guided trips: caving, heli-caving/heli-sightseeing/heli-adventure combination, and heli-sightseeing. **Location:** Scheduled trips to a number of caves on Vancouver Island, starting from Gold River. Gold River is 90 kilometres west of Campbell River, 240 kilometres from Nanaimo, and 350 kilometres from Victoria. Customized trips starting from most locations on Vancouver Island to more than a thousand caves. **Level of difficulty:** Beginner, intermediate, and advanced. Participants should be reasonably fit. **Cost/what provided:** Scheduled caving trips from $12 per person; scheduled heli-caving/heli-sightseeing/heli-adventure combination trips from $125 per person; includes guide service, lighting equipment, and head protection. Heli-sightseeing trips: variable rates, depending on trip's duration and destination. Customized trip and group rates. **In the adventure travel operator's own words:** "Caves are among Canada's most endangered spaces. Explore some of the very best limestone scenery and caves in the country. Discover the world inside Vancouver Island—"The Island of Caves"—with expert guides. A cave tour can offer even the most experienced outdoor enthusiast an opportunity to explore a landscape unlike any other on earth. If you've always wanted to visit a cave, why not take advantage of this unique opportunity to turn your vacation into a fascinating adventure. We will go out of our way to make sure your underground journey is an experience you'll never forget."

Section 50: Guided caving and heli-caving

Cross-references

Island Sauvage Guiding Company—Vancouver Island; p. 18

Mount Revelstoke and Glacier National Parks—Mount Revelstoke and Glacier national parks in the Columbia Mountains between Golden and Revelstoke; p. 20

Nimmo Bay Heli-Ventures—northern Vancouver Island and nearby mainland areas; p. 86

Section 51: Guided gold panning and prospecting

Cross-references

Big Bar Guest Ranch—the Cariboo area near Clinton; p. 74

Bracewell's Alpine Wilderness Adventures—the Chilcotin Plateau; p. 78

Section 52: Guided hot springs tours

Cross-references

Iskutine Lodge—northwestern B.C.; p. 16

Kermodei Wilderness Tours—the northern coast of B.C.; the Inside Passage area near Kitimat; p. 23

Pemberton Helicopters—the Coast Mountains near Whistler; p. 44

Nature Connection—the Queen Charlotte Islands; the Inside Passage of B.C.; Johnstone Strait; Robson Bight; p. 83

Jasper Adventure Centre—Jasper National Park; p. 93

Alpine Adventure Tours

Doug Banner
Box 48903
Vancouver, BC V7X 1A8
(604) 683-0209
Fax: (604) 683-6037

Scheduled and customized sightseeing tours via train, bus, and/or boat. **Location:** The Vancouver/Whistler area. Examples of trips: one trip is by the Royal Hudson steam train from North Vancouver to Squamish and by bus to Whistler, returning by passenger rail to North Vancouver, with free time in Whistler; another trip is by the MV*Britannia* coastal cruiseship from Vancouver to Squamish and by bus to Whistler, returning by passenger rail to North Vancouver, with free time in Whistler; a third trip is by the Royal Hudson steam train from North Vancouver to Squamish and by bus to Whistler, returning by bus to Squamish and by the MV *Britannia* coastal cruiseship to Vancouver, with a stay of one or more nights in Whistler. **Time:** Between June 30 and September 30. **Accommodation:** Hotels in Whistler Village.

Cross-references

Hammerhead Mountain Bike/Scenic Tours—the Badlands, near Drumheller; p. 34

Timberwolf Tours—northern Alberta; the Rocky Mountains; the Kootenays; p. 41

Jasper Adventure Centre—Jasper National Park; p. 93

Gang Ranch

Gang Ranch Post Office
Gang Ranch, BC V0K 1N0
(604) 459-7923
Fax: (604) 459-2624

A million-acre working ranch—the Gang Ranch—with a guest house, horse boarding, and unguided activities including horseback riding, bicycling, hiking, and photography. Guests bring their own horses and/or bicycles. **Location:** Near Clinton. **Some highlights:** The world's second largest herd of California bighorn sheep. **Cost/what provided:** $85 to $150 per person per day, depending on room and meals requested. **Extras for additional cost:** Boarding for guests' horses. **Accommodation:** The guest house has three rooms and a shared bath. **In the adventure travel operator's own words:** "The ranch is huge, it's historic, and it's a cowboy outfit. Its history rolls back for 150 rich and gritty years. Today it covers a million acres of prime bunch grass, rugged timber, canyons, sagebrush, and rivers. It's a challenging, sometimes unforgiving, piece of the earth, not suited for the meek or faint-hearted individual. We look forward to sharing a unique experience with you."

Mountain Trek Fitness Retreat and Health Spa

Wendy Pope
Box 1352
Ainsworth Hot Springs, BC V0G 1A0
Phone and fax: (604) 229-5636
Toll-free for reservations: 1-800-661-5161

A fitness retreat and health spa in the Selkirk Mountains near Nelson and Castlegar, overlooking Kootenay Lake, a five-minute walk from Ainsworth Hot Springs. Return transportation from Castlegar airport at no additional cost. Activities include hiking, yoga, massage, weight training, exercise classes, and fasting programs. Ainsworth Hot Springs is a five-minute walk from the lodge. Lodge accommodation facilities include ten private bedrooms and bathrooms for a maximum of sixteen guests, a lounge with fireplace, an outdoor Jacuzzi, a sauna, a weight room, an exercise studio, and laundry facilities. **Cost/what provided:** Six-day hiking programs from $1,550 to $1,825 per person, including use of all facilities, accommodation, meals, six mountain hikes, three massages, six yoga/stretch classes, and return transportation from Castlegar airport. Six-day fasting programs from $750 to $1,100 per person, including use of all facilities, accommodation, educational lectures, five yoga/stretch classes, walks, a massage, fasting treatments, and return transportation from Castlegar airport. Longer fasting/cleansing programs and two-week hiking/fasting combination programs are available. **In the adventure travel operator's own words:** "Imagine waking to the sound of the mountains at dawn—the wind in the pines, the cry of an osprey, the faint hush of a glacier-fed stream. Imagine spending your day without appointments or deadlines. Hiking through alpine meadows teeming with flowers. Breathing air so pure it exhilarates the lungs. Imagine a week completely devoted to your physical and mental well-being with a vigorous hiking program, a healthy selection of tempting meals, a daily massage, and the luxury of carefree slumber. Don't just imagine a healthier you—become that person."

Hollyhock

Greg Osoba
Box 127
Manson's Landing
Cortes Island, BC   V0P 1K0
Toll-free: 1-800-933-6339
Fax: (604) 935-6424

A health retreat on Cortes Island, 150 kilometres north of Vancouver, with scheduled guided trips, outdoor activities, outdoor camps for children, and seminars and workshops in practical, creative, and healing arts. Over eighty seminars and workshops between March and October; accommodation year round. Seminar and workshop topics include natural history, health, fitness, meditation, massage, music, literature, art, and spirituality. Guided trips include sea kayaking, sea canoeing, sailing, and nature walks. Other activities include rowing, swimming, jogging, exercise classes, and sea kayaking instruction. **Cost/what provided:** Weekend trip: $119 to $309 per person, depending on season and occupancy. Seven-day trip: $309 to $969 per person, depending on season and occupancy. Trips include accommodation, meals, guided walks, natural history tours, outdoor hot tub, Saturday night entertainment, and a bodywork or skin care session. Daily rates for accommodation and meals only: $44 to $134, depending on season and occupancy. Children's and group rates. Visa, MasterCard. **Extras for additional cost:** Seminars, workshops, outdoor programs and some activities. **In the adventure travel operator's own words:** "Hollyhock is the holiday you've always dreamed of, in a spectacular wilderness setting. The combination of world-class presenters, caring and supportive staff, and unparalleled environment rejuvenates your body and mind and rekindles your spirit. You'll find plenty of opportunities for companionship. Whatever you choose, you'll come away from Hollyhock renewed. Join us for a holiday that heals."

The Hills Health and Guest Ranch

Pat Corbett
C–26
108 Ranch, BC V0K 2Z0
(604) 791-5225
Fax: (604) 791-6384

A health spa and fitness resort on a ranch in the Cariboo, near 100 Mile House, offering scheduled guided activities including hiking, horseback riding, and hay rides; services including massages, facials, herbal wraps, and manicures; aerobics classes; and barbecues. **In the adventure travel operator's own words:** "Your day can be planned to include a range of choices, from attending one of many aerobics classes to going on a half-day cowboy breakfast ride. You can join one of our two daily guided hikes and then luxuriate with a massage, facial, herbal wrap, and manicure. Later, get ready for an old-fashioned horse-drawn hayride party to our Indian teepee, where you will join our entertainers for an evening of fun and laughter you'll never forget."

Cross-references

Lake Louise Inn—Banff National Park; p. 115
The Edgewater—Whistler; p. 117

Vancouver Natural History Society
Other trips offered by this adventure travel operator,
pages 91 and 112.

Box 3021, Main Post Office
Vancouver, BC V6B 3X5
(604) 525-9498
Fax: (604) 527-5095

Summer camps in a number of locations, including Garibaldi Park, Chilko Lake, Waterton Lakes, Cinnabar Basin, and Manning Park. Each camp emphasizes the natural history of a particular wilderness area. **More information:** Families with children are welcome to participate in most camps.

Cross-references

Canadian Adventure Safaris—children's wilderness survival camp in the Rocky Mountains; p. 73

Hollyhock—children's outdoor camp on Cortes Island in the northern Gulf Islands; p. 107

Fair Winds Sailing School

1140 Kildonan Place SW
Calgary, AB T2V 4B1
(403) 252-7578

B.C. associate: Maple Bay Yacht Services
Toll-free voice mail in B.C.: (604) 975-3181

Sailing courses, bare boat yacht charters, and scheduled and customized guided sailing trips. **Location:** The Gulf Islands, between Vancouver Island and the mainland. Basic route is a hundred-mile circuit of the Gulf Islands, with overnight harbour stops. Trips begin and end at Maple Bay Marina on Vancouver Island, near Duncan; return transportation from Victoria or Nanaimo airport or ferry terminal at no additional cost. **Level of difficulty:** Basic, intermediate, and advanced sailing courses. No previous sailing experience necessary for basic course. Intermediate and advanced courses available for those with suitable qualifications. **Time:** Between May 1 and September 30. One-week courses start at 4:00 p.m. Sundays and finish at 9:00 a.m. Saturdays. Other times by arrangement. **Cost/what provided:** Sailing courses, $700 to $800 per person. Includes instruction; accommodation; beverages; meals, including Friday dinner in a luxury restaurant; and return transportation from Victoria or Nanaimo airport or ferry terminal. Guided trips and bare boat yacht charters: call for rates. Cash, cheques; no credit cards. Rates for multiple bookings. **Group size:** Maximum of four students plus instructor per vessel. **Accommodation:** On 33- to 35-foot yachts. **In the adventure travel operator's own words:** "Learn an outdoor skill you can practise for a lifetime, while you vacation in one of the world's ten greatest cruising areas. Our mature, friendly instructors are certified by the Canadian Yachting Association, and our courses meet standards set by that organization."

South Island Sailtraining

4098 Raymond Street North
Victoria, BC V8Z 4L6
Phone and fax: (604) 479-6604

Sailing courses on scheduled and customized guided sailing trips. Shore-based sailing courses. Other activities on the trips: birdwatching, marine mammal viewing, diving, tide water exploration, photography, and swimming. **Location:** Southern Vancouver Island and the Gulf Islands. Trips start from Victoria. **Level of difficulty:** Courses for novice to experienced sailors. **Time:** Sailing courses on sailing trips, between April and October, are typically five days and four nights. Winter and summer shore-based courses: call for information. **Cost/what provided:** Sailing courses on sailing trips, $520 per person. Groups of two to four students per vessel. Students participate in meal preparation on board. Shore-based courses, $230 per person. Cash, cheques. **Extras for additional cost:** International Sail and Power Association documentation and manual, $15 each. Accommodation and meals for shore-based courses. **In the instructor's own words:** "Our courses, from basic to advanced, are taught to International Sail and Power Association Standards. We offer knowledgeable and friendly instruction in seamanship and sailing in a total marine environment, where students are encouraged to participate in boat handling to an extent in keeping with their desires and experience."

Vancouver Natural History Society

Other trips offered by this adventure travel operator,
pages 91 and 110.

Box 3021, Main Post Office
Vancouver, BC V6B 3X5
(604) 525-9498
Fax: (604) 527-5095

Monthly evening programs on all aspects of natural history, including wilderness conservation, marine biology, astronomy, botany, forestry, and zoology. **Location:** The Vancouver Museum and Planetarium auditorium. **Time:** Between October and May, once per month.

Canada West Mountain School (a division of the Federation of Mountain Clubs of B.C.)

336—1367 West Broadway
Vancouver, BC   V6H 4A9
(604) 737-3053
Fax: (604) 738-7175

Scheduled and customized mountain skills courses and guided trips. In summer: rock climbing, mountaineering, and backpacking. In winter: avalanche safety, ice climbing, ski touring, telemarking, and snow camping. Guided peak climbs year round. **Location:** Southwestern B.C., the Coast Mountains, the Selkirk Mountains, and the Yukon. Trips start at various locations in B.C. **Some highlights:** Personal coaching, low student to instructor ratio, high alpine camps, multi-day ski traverses, peak ascents, and glacier travel. **Level of difficulty:** Courses and trips from beginner to advanced, according to participants' needs and experience. **Time:** Year round. Trips from two days to two weeks. **Cost/what provided:** Two-day courses, $125 to $175 per person, including instruction and park permits. Some guided trips include food, camping equipment, and transportation to trip site. **Accommodation:** Tents or public cabins. **In the adventure travel operator's own words:** "Our school has been committed to providing first-rate mountain safety instruction since 1982. Our comprehensive program is guaranteed to offer something for climbers, hikers, and ski tourers of all abilities. Instructors are qualified, and guided trips are led by Association of Canadian Mountain Guides (ACMG) members. We are a registered non-profit association. Your safety is our priority."

Cross-references

Island Sauvage Guiding Company—surfing; p. 18

Northern Lights Alpine Recreation—technical ropework for mountain climbing; p. 29

Island Sauvage Guiding Company—avalanche awareness; awareness for heli-access terrain; snowboarding; p. 42

Pemberton Soaring Centre—glider piloting; p. 48

Geoff Evans Kayak Centre—sea kayaking; p. 50

Tofino Sea Kayaking Company—sea kayaking; p. 52

Ecomarine Ocean Kayak Centre—sea kayaking; p. 54

Island Sauvage Guiding Company—sea kayaking; p. 55

REO Rafting Adventures/Nahatlatch River Resort—river rafting; p. 65

Canadian Adventure Safaris—wilderness survival for children; p. 73

Bracewell's Alpine Wilderness Adventures—horseback riding; outdoor survival; p. 78

Mountain Trek Fitness Retreat and Health Spa—health and fitness; p. 106

Hollyhock—sea kayaking; natural history; p. 107

The Hills Health and Guest Ranch—health and fitness; p. 108

The Edgewater—health; p. 117

Lake Louise Inn

210 Village Road
Mail: Box 209
Lake Louise, AB T0L 1E0
(403) 522-3791
Toll-free in Canada and the U.S.: 1-800-661-9237
Fax: (403) 522-2018

An inn providing information on adventure travel activities and offering health and lifestyle retreat packages and ski packages. The information on adventure travel activities covers the services of a number of adventure travel operators in the Banff/Lake Louise area of the Rocky Mountains who offer a variety of guided activities including heli-hiking, heli-sightseeing, hiking, whitewater rafting, wilderness and flatwater canoeing, horseback riding, heli-skiing, downhill skiing, cross-country skiing, dogsledding, and snowshoeing. The health and lifestyle retreat packages are four to six days. The ski packages include three or more ski trips at the nearby ski areas of Lake Louise, Sunshine Village, and Mystic Ridge/Mount Norquay; lift tickets; accommodation; and, for the Lake Louise ski area, return bus transportation from the inn. Return bus transportation to the other ski areas is available. The inn has two hundred and twenty-two rooms, suites, and family units; rates are $50 to $195, depending on season and type of room. Some rooms have queen-sized beds and balconies. Each suite has a kitchen, a fireplace, and a balcony. Each family unit has a kitchen and a fireplace. The inn has a restaurant with a patio and barbecue (summer only), a licensed lounge, a gazebo where barbecued meals are served (summer only), a pub, a heated indoor pool, a whirlpool, and a sauna. In summer, the Rocky Mountain Shakespeare Theatre Company performs two plays and the Alberta Birds of Prey Centre has an educational exhibit at the ski area.

Far Side of the Mountain

Eric Duerkson and Alexa Collings
55 Castleridge Boulevard NE
Mail: Box 80026
Calgary, AB T3J 3L6
(403) 293-5464
Toll-free for reservations: 1-800-999-4616
Fax: (403) 293-5624
For ski conditions: (403) 280-4200

Information on and reservations for ski resorts in B.C. and Alberta and guided and unguided skiing trips in B.C. and Alberta. Guided trips: heli-, snowcat, and downhill skiing. Unguided trips: downhill skiing. **Level of difficulty:** Beginner to advanced. **Cost/what provided:** Rates vary, depending on trip's destination and duration. No booking fees. **In the adventure travel planner's own words:** "We have been planning custom ski vacations for groups and individuals since 1978. We invite you to sit back and relax and let us do the planning for your next ski adventure."

The Edgewater

Melissa and Diederik Wolsak
8841 Highway 99
Mail: Box 369
Whistler, BC V0N 1B0
(604) 932-0688
Fax: (604) 932-0686

A waterfront resort at Whistler providing an information and reservation service for scheduled and customized guided trips, downhill ski and golf packages, ski and snowboard rentals, and, in early spring and fall, mental and physical health workshops. The guided trips include downhill skiing, heli–downhill skiing, ski-lift ski touring, heli–ski touring, horseback riding, whitewater and flatwater canoeing, whitewater rafting, alpine meadow hiking, ski-lift hiking, heli-hiking, mountaineering, rock climbing, nature tours, ski-lift nature tours, heli–glacier sightseeing tours, heli–glacier landing tours, mountain biking, ski-lift mountain biking, airplane and heli–mountain biking, paragliding, airplane freshwater fishing, heli–freshwater fishing, and airplane and heli-sightseeing. The resort is 3 kilometres north of Whistler Village on 45 acres of land on Green Lake. Float plane access. Twelve rooms with private baths, some with an adjacent room and private deck. **Room rates/what provided:** $80 to $215, depending on season and type of room. Includes Continental breakfast, sherry, chocolates, appetizers, and flowers. King-sized, queen-sized, or twin beds. Outdoor hot tub. Lounge with fireplace. **In the adventure travel planner's own words:** "Our resort offers a civilized base for unparalleled outdoor activities. Dramatic views of Whistler, Blackcomb, and other mountains, undisturbed privacy, gourmet dinners, unique wine selections, and pampered comfort prepare our guests for some of the finest adventure experiences to be found anywhere."

A Selection of Books Published by Gordon Soules Book Publishers